THE LONG TERM STARTS TOMORROW

Nigel Lake

Frog Publishing

Published by Frog Publishing, Sydney, Australia

Cover by ASP Graphic Design

Typeset in Bembo by Frog Publishing
Printed and bound in Australia by Griffin Press

A CIP catalogue record for this book is available
from The National Library of Australia

ISBN 978 - 0992 - 36060 - 3

WWW.NIGELLAKE.COM
WWW.TWITTER.COM/NIGEL_LAKE

Dedication and recognition

No idea is born in a vacuum, nor can any book truly be the work of a single person. Both need to be nurtured and enriched through conversation, challenge and reflection.

There are many people who have made a significant contribution to bringing this book to life, through their friendship, ideas and enthusiasm. They are too many to name here and these words are a mark of my respect for them and appreciation of their time, effort, thought and passion.

Everyone at Pottinger (the strategic and financial advisory firm which I co-founded a decade ago) has been incredibly supportive on many levels. It has been – and continues to be – a real privilege to work with such a talented and creative team. I am enormously appreciative of their input and patience.

As I reflect on the two years it has taken to develop the original concepts that are embodied in "The Long Term Starts Tomorrow", I dedicate this book to all those that have inspired me to think about how better to connect the "now" with the long term.

In particular, I thank my amazing wife, business partner and mentor Cassandra, who gave me the gift of courage and confidence to write this book – and indeed to develop and grow in ways that I had never imagined were possible. She also booked the requisite mountain lodge and sent me away to finish writing – I am not sure who was more delighted!

And I also thank my children Alexander, Katherine and William, who have each provided endless inspiration through their energy, love and fresh, uninhibited thinking.

Foreword

When you build a fire, it isn't where you put the sticks that matters, it's where you put the holes. The holes let the air circulate, carrying oxygen to feed the fire. If you pack the sticks too tightly, the fire soon dies. If you pack them too loosely, or with no care for how they are arranged, the kindling will burn out and the logs will never catch.

It's the same with businesses and most other organisations. You need the right mix of infrastructure and freedom, or your fire will never burn brightly. This book has been written for leaders across business and government and beyond, who seek to make a real difference to their organisation and who may be struggling to see or deliver their vision in a risky and rapidly changing world. The thinking applies as much to nations and not for profit organisations as it does to companies, so replace one with another as you read.

The application of scientific method and economic theory to business since World War Two has brought much needed rigour to decision-making. But it has also stifled innovation and encouraged tactics so short term that some of the world's largest companies have been destroyed in a matter of months or even weeks. Happily, the opposite is also true. The internet giants of today ignored short term revenues and profits completely and instead created businesses that would be valuable in the future – a long term plan unlocked by the right short term focus.

These outcomes show that there are fundamental flaws in conventional business thinking and decision-making. The tools we are using today have proved to be remarkably poor at identifying star performers and avoiding corporate disasters over even relatively short time periods. By exposing the reasons for these failings, and providing rigorous new ways to examine how best to unlock future profitability and value, I hope to set organisations (and even personal investment portfolios!) free so that they can emulate the growth and inventiveness and success of the world's greatest companies. And I have suggested a simple, incisive methodology to test whether your current medium to long term thinking is likely to be found wanting within just a few years.

There are also moral issues that we should consider seriously. If you doubt this, and you are an ardent believer in the power of financial analysis and discounted cash flow models, then apply these methodologies to your family. Discount (in a financial sense) the value of the lives of your children and grandchildren. You should find the results horrifying.

And of course even the best laid fire, if it burns too brightly, will burn out before morning. You wake up and find there are only cold ashes and not even a glowing ember remains. For many of the largest, most successful organisations, their most fearsome competitor is internal, embodied in the self-satisfaction and over-confidence that is all too common in long established market leaders. If it takes hold, this supremacy gene leads to a sickness that is so severe that there may simply be no cure other than corporate death or the electric shock of a takeover.

Even if the supremacy gene can be bred out, vested interests, industry structures, business cultures, linear thinking and over-regulation inhibit innovation and straightjacket the most successful organisations. Short-termism may be successful in the short term – in industries with high barriers to entry for example. But over time, pretty much every organisation that doesn't evolve will die.

These challenges are well understood in the academic world, but in day to day corporate and government life, they are either ignored or brushed aside as too great a challenge to tackle.

The accelerating pace of change is even more significant. For millennia, humans have learned that doing things the same way – the way that worked yesterday and last month and last year – is safer than trying something new. This is "instinct". The best place to build your camp and light your fire is the river bank that folklore records has never flooded. This is "experience". But in a world where an entire new global industry worth a trillion dollars can emerge in a decade, and take 50% market share from the incumbents of yesterday, instinct and experience may no longer work. This implies that an inflexion point is rapidly approaching, after which doing things differently becomes safer than sticking with what you know.

To embrace this requires a truly profound change to the human psyche. Animal and human instinct is born out of hundreds of thousands of years of experience that doing things in a proven way is safer than trying something new. So it is natural than the average voter or shareholder or bank depositor puts more emphasis on short term rewards. So I've explored how and why this obsession with near term returns works out *worse* for them over the longer term.

Finally, creating the right culture is one of the greatest opportunities for leaders, whether in business, politics, sport or the not for profit sector. Whilst this is never easy, change *can* be achieved and is essential to our hopes for economic and social prosperity. Many countries are labouring under massive debts, not to mention the silent cancer of un-funded retirement benefits. Together, we must find new and significantly better ways to tackle the problems of the day. Ten thousand years of history show that to do this we must *think differently* – approaches that are tried and tested will simply not deliver the innovation that is required.

Like a frog in the proverbial cool pan of water, there is a real risk that human decision-making will remain dangerously focussed on indicators that are too short term in nature and that we won't see the opportunities that lie ahead in time. As a result, we won't choose the safer, more profitable path.

So to everyone, I say this. Help the frog jump out of the pan! Without a crisis to drive rapid decisions, humans are all too often very resistant to change. With the pace of invention continuing to accelerate, change must become a more natural part of our lives. So don't just dream of a better future – think differently and act to make it happen. Speak respectfully of course, but if your colleagues don't like what you are saying, then you will know that you are working in the wrong place.

And in every decision you make, remember that the long term starts tomorrow. How you lay and tend the fire today will determine whether you wake up to cold ashes, or are part of an organisation or community that continues to grow and thrive over the long term.

Contents

1. Do you have $100bn in your garage?......................... 1

    The next Google or yesterday's hero?................................1

    From garage to global leader in just ten years....................3

    Would you even notice a $100 billion opportunity?............5

    The birth of economic rationalism 6

    The siren call of endless growth – how long till you hit the rocks? ..9

    The long term starts tomorrow (part 1) 11

2. The Two Percent challenge.......................... 16

    Short term gain, long term pain......................................16

    Would you discount your family? 19

    So where's the flaw? 23

    No-one ever got fired for hiring IBM..............................26

    Flirting with permanency – introducing the 2% challenge............27

    Do you want to play Russian roulette, corporate style?...................30

3. Burn the base case: welcoming complexity.............. 33

    Could your weakest competitor outgrow you 400x? 33

    Abandoning the animal preference for the status quo 36

    What do you do when the average never happens?........................39

    100% wrong: guaranteed!..41

    Long term growth, short term insanity.............................43

    The limits to (compound) growth.....................................45

    Long term value in a short term world 47

    Change is slow, but revolutions happen overnight 49

    Embracing risk and welcoming uncertainty 52

4. Casting off the chains of the free market 53

    If the free market is so efficient, why doesn't it work?......................53

    The white goods conundrum 54

    Have you built barriers to success into your business? 56

Choose the rules – beware the game 63

Let's make our club more exclusive 64

Are you legislating for gain or pain? 67

Incumbents 4, Innovators 0 69

How long would you wait for freedom? 73

5. The supremacy gene 76

Can't they see the writing on the wall? 76

Great business – shame about the leverage 80

Betting against the house – and winning 82

The battle of the titans 84

Corporate DNA testing 87

The supremacy gene 88

Success breeds success (and more pain?) 91

Consumers and politicians are vulnerable too 95

Kill or cure? 96

6. The energy revolution 98

Time to look in the mirror 98

Good things never last forever 99

If you want to plan for the long term, why not start now? 101

Beyond financial Armageddon: the world of illusory growth 105

Stop thinking of elephants 106

Is there that much to lose? 110

Will your company miss the world's next great revolution? 111

7. An obituary for financial rationalism 116

The origin of capitalism 116

The birth of the corporation 117

Globalisation and the dawn of empires 119

Industrial conglomerates 120

Enter Modigliani and Miller 121

The lost decade 122

Economic theory finally reaches the boardroom.........................124

The Siren call of compound growth 129

Business schools and the birth of financial rationalism................130

Financial warlords...134

Where to from here?...136

8. You've escaped, so don't look back! 138

Welcome to the accidental present...............................138

Blowing with the corporate winds of destiny 141

Disruptive innovation or predictable change?......................143

How clear is the crystal ball?...................................145

Switching on the innovation radar 151

9. Never mind the strategy, where are we going?........ 154

The accidental circumnavigation of Sark..........................154

Corporate idol worship 158

Guilty as charged: choosing incremental inefficiency 161

Can you hear your company's own death knell? 163

That's a beautiful map, but where are we going? 164

Crystal balls 101: building a truly insightful financial model.......167

The perils of linear thinking 172

Ignoring the "no" in innovation 175

10. Epilogue: Saving Jorgen's frog:............................ 179

Where did all the growth go? 179

Saving Jorgen's Frog...181

The long term starts tomorrow (part 2) 184

Small selfish steps 188

Embrace madness! 191

1. Do you have $100bn in your garage?

THE NEXT GOOGLE OR YESTERDAY'S HERO?

Which do you think are the world's greatest companies? The list of iconic corporate leaders of today is as rich as ever, spanning old and new industries, dynastic empires and recent start-ups, West and East. Google and Facebook have created value through connecting information and people on the internet. Mobile technology, like that delivered by Apple and Samsung, has changed the way people live and work. Mining giants such as BHP and Rio are harvesting mineral and resource wealth from the earth. Leaders such as Baosteel and Tata in the rapidly growing economies of China and India are creating significant value in manufacturing and services.

Meanwhile long established companies such as GE, ExxonMobil, Procter & Gamble and DuPont are amongst the leaders their industries globally – all of them joined the Dow Jones Industrial Average over 75 years ago. And of the world's 50 richest individuals, over 20% are associated with fashion retailing businesses.

Despite this diversity, if you look by revenues and profits and value, a substantial element of the world's largest companies are resources companies – four of the five most profitable companies fall into this category. These are old economy companies, whose long term futures face some significant challenges as a result of the commitment by many nations around the world to take significant action to reduce carbon emissions. These companies have been around for a long time, and have been successful in preserving their position in the market value pecking order.

Meanwhile, the world's most valuable company is Apple, and according to Forbes the six most powerful brands globally are Apple, Microsoft, Coca Cola, IBM, Google and Intel. Notably five are technology companies, and all are from the USA. This is a telling illustration of the importance of innovation in *creating* value.

Whoever is in your own personal top ten, it is more than likely that at least a handful of these will not have existed ten to fifteen years ago. Others have been around for much longer, but have been completely transformed over the space of a decade or two.

There is nothing new in this invention and reinvention of businesses. Ever since the emergence of the world's first company – the Dutch East India Company, which issued stock in 1602 – organisations have sought to build their size and profitability. National and global leaders have wielded significant power, in economic, social and political terms, and have been responsible for shaping the growth and fortune of nations. At its peak, the Dutch East India Company was more powerful than many countries, sending nearly a million Europeans to work in its trade with Asia, more than the rest of Europe combined, on a fleet of nearly 5,000 ships. The company generated substantial profits from its monopoly on the spice trade from the likes of countries now known as Indonesia.

These figures remain impressive to this day. Even by country, the world's largest shipping fleet in 2012 is that of Japan, with fewer than 4,000 vessels. But like too many once great companies, the Dutch East India Company suffered an ignominious end in bankruptcy and was wound up in the year 1800.

FROM GARAGE TO GLOBAL LEADER IN JUST TEN YEARS

What *is* new is the speed at which corporate fortunes can be made. The most obvious example is Google, which celebrates its 15th birthday in 2013 and has created $1.7 billion a month of shareholder value since its formation. This is far more than recent "pop and flop" IPO companies such as Zynga, which reached a peak valuation of some $10.7 billion three months after its IPO (57 months after formation), equating to just $187 million per month (and it's subsequently fallen in value by some 80%).

Revolutionary growth is not just the preserve of start-ups. Apple was 20 years old and at a corporate death's door in 1997, before the extraordinary turnaround driven by the return of Steve Jobs and just four core products. The launch of the iPod in 2001 marked a shift in Apple's focus away from computer and software manufacturing toward consumer electronics. In just 15 years, the company's market value grew from $2.5 billion to become the world's first $600 billion company on 10th April 2012, a spectacular compound growth rate of nearly 45% a year.

Indeed companies such as Apple, Google, Facebook and others have created their own markets through imagining and creating entirely new products or services that have become household names and household items almost overnight.

It's important to emphasise that examples such as these are not confined simply to the internet sector. At different points in time, organisations such as Nokia and Samsung have transformed themselves from drab industrial also-rans to global leaders. IBM once sold commercial scales and punch card tabulators, graduating to mainframe computers – now it is one of the world's leading software, consulting and IT services companies. Monsanto was the purveyor of saccharine, and is now a world leader in seed technologies. Fortune Brands originally focussed on tobacco, and now sells hardware, home furnishings and golf clubs. 3M made sandpaper, and is now more famous for Post-It notes.

Meanwhile, Nokia started out selling paper and lumber in the nineteenth century, used hydro-electric power in its saw mills, and sold surplus electricity to external customers. It then diversified into rubber (from trees), manufacturing rubber boots, tyres and insulated electrical cables. From there, it diversified further into consumer electronics, including televisions and even semi-conductors, before entering the telecommunications sector and eventually becoming the clear world leader in 2G mobile phones and network equipment. The journey since has been a somewhat chequered one, ending in the sale of Nokia's devices business to Microsoft in 2012 for a small fraction of its year 2000 value.

What is also new is the sheer scale and connectivity of the global leaders of today. Companies such as Facebook and Google each have around a billion customers, and their products and brands are known to the majority of people in the world. Consumer activism, online interaction and social media have all placed more power in the hands of consumers and created ever greater commercial opportunities and risks. This increased corporate, financial and social dynamism has created enormous challenges for many long established and highly successful companies.

Indeed, of the world's ten most valuable listed companies, eight are truly global corporations with a substantial impact in most countries. This includes organisations such as Apple, Chevron, Exxon Mobil, GE, Google, Johnson & Johnson, General Electric and Microsoft. Meanwhile Chinese names are rising upwards rapidly, with both PetroChina and ICBC now in the top ten.

Without a doubt the world of today is dramatically more dynamic than the world of 1800. Corporate and national decisions are made against a substantially more uncertain outlook, where anticipating the likely environment in five years time has become exceptionally challenging. Decisions made using base case forecasts and in the light of a few hypothetical upside and downside scenarios are increasingly risky, because they are not likely to reflect a realistic or complete view of all the real world scenarios that are likely to occur in practice. This implies that fundamentally new approaches to decision-making are essential.

WOULD YOU EVEN NOTICE A $100 BILLION OPPORTUNITY?

The stories of corporate glory and destruction make great reading and intriguing case studies. Many of them also serve to highlight that key aspects of business thinking no longer work in the modern world. If you had been sitting in the garage with Bill Gates or Steve Jobs, and you pulled out your shiny new business school valuation toolkit, would you ever have seriously considered scenarios where you contemplated a $100 billion valuation or more?

For nearly everyone the answer will be no, for some simple reasons. Firstly, you would never have believed the growth rates that were required. Secondly, the real inflexion in valuation lay more than a decade after original launch and would never have been explored in your models. Thirdly, the main leap in value for a company like Apple was created through a change in business model two decades after formation which allowed the creation of a series of new markets, each generating hundreds of billions of dollars a year of revenues globally.

If you'd been offered the opportunity to invest in these companies during their first few years, would you have done so? Would you have seen the probability of enormous wealth creation and world-changing innovation? Or would you have seen the risk and thought that it was safer to wait a while until the technology was better proven?

Every day, large organisations defer decisions to make investments that might secure long term growth and prosperity because there is too much risk. Very often, this actually means that the risks aren't well understood, or the decision-makers simply don't have the tool set to grapple with the trade off between risks and returns. And all too often, the comfort of the status quo and industry leadership mean that companies hunker down and ignore the warning signs that the rules of the game in their industry are about to change.

In other words, there is clear evidence that the basic tools that are used to evaluate both growth strategies and new opportunities have some fundamental flaws. They place too much emphasis on the near term, *creating* risk and *destroying value.* So how can you address these challenges? What tools can you use to make sure that your medium to long term plans will survive these dramatic inflexion points?

THE BIRTH OF ECONOMIC RATIONALISM

Around the world, in companies and financial institutions and Government departments, significant decisions have been based on a particular type of economic rationalism for at least the last twenty to thirty years. This new financial religion was born out of Modigliani and Miller's theorems of capital structure, and was seized on by business and financial users seeking reliable, objective and quantitative methods for corporate decision-making. Discounted cash flow valuations, leverage and capital structure optimisation became business buzzwords and provided a robust and intellectually sound justification for M&A transactions, deployment of capital and Government policy.

The late 1980s and early 1990s saw widespread conversion to this way of thinking in the business world, at first on Wall Street, and then in the City of London and beyond. In the early days, thinking continued to evolve, with the techniques adapted for use in industries with additional constraints to be considered. This included sectors with unusual capital structures or regulatory requirements, including banks, insurers and regulated utility companies, as well as the more straightforward but detailed modelling required for highly leveraged transactions.

I had the rare privilege of participating in these developments first hand in the early to mid 1990s in London, working at Barings, then arguably the leading investment banking business in Europe. We were at the forefront of adapting the basic discounted cash flow techniques to a range of specialist industries, including financial services, utilities and infrastructure. Endless hours of late night modelling and heated discussions about the technical and academic merits of alternative approaches were fascinating. The change to how major acquisitions and projects were assessed was dramatic, and the sophistication of decision-making increased notably in the space of a few years.

What is even more striking, however, is that these techniques have barely evolved at all in the subsequent fifteen years. The financial models I see today, produced by leading investment banks around the world, are almost identical in methodology and approach to those that we wrote in the mid 1990s. And yet the world is dramatically more uncertain than it was in the mid 1990s, and the overnight success stories and disasters of the last decade show all too clearly that these techniques are, at best, unreliable.

Today, many in the business and financial worlds hold an unshakeable belief in the rigour of discounted cash flow valuations and they are routinely used to inform many business decisions. Most of the disciples who worship at the altar of financial rationalism are aware that the techniques have limitations and drawbacks, and have found techniques to accommodate these weaknesses. But from my experience, relatively few have thought deeply about the implications of their methods.

From a typical business perspective, financial rationalism feels like an entirely intuitive approach. But it simply doesn't work. There are many examples of overnight success stories and dramatic corporate collapses from the last two decades of business history which provide tangible evidence that there must be fundamental flaws in these methodologies, or at the very least how they are being used. It would be easy to dismiss these successes and failures as examples of heroic leadership, visionary insight or just plain good luck.

But businesses need much more than this if they are to have the tools to make better decisions. This is an uncomfortable challenge. Any replacement for these fundamental tools needs to be financially rigorous, but somehow must also deal much more effectively with uncertainty and ensuring better longer term outcomes.

THE SIREN CALL OF ENDLESS GROWTH – HOW LONG TILL YOU HIT THE ROCKS?

Companies and governments and shareholders and voters have all grown used to relatively high rates of compound growth over the last fifty years. Some of the world's largest companies have committed at various times to achieving 10% or 15% or even 20% compound growth in shareholder value year after year. Others have talked about doubling shareholder value over five or four or even three years (that's a 26% compound growth rate). These figures won't sound at all unreasonable to most in the business world, certainly at the lower end.

But stop for a moment and think about what these growth rates mean over more than just a few years. The effects of compounding are far from intuitive for most people. The population of the USA was 76,094,000 in 1900. If the population had grown at 10% a year, by 2012 the population would have reached 3.3 trillion – and remember the world's population today is only seven billion. Again, using a 10% growth rate, New York State's population would have grown from 7.3 million to about 316 billion over the same period.

Even 5% compound growth would have been dramatic, yielding a US population of 18 billion, with 1.7 billion of those people living in New York. In comparison, the world's population has grown at little more than 1% a year on average over the last thousand years, and world economic growth has averaged less than 2%.

So economy wide growth assumptions of even 10% a year are entirely unrealistic over anything other than relatively short time horizons.

There are, of course, industries, where much higher growth rates in underlying measures of business volume have been observed, in some cases for decades at a time. In Australia, internet data traffic (and its forerunners) has increased at a compound rate of close to 35% a year since 1980. If the country's population had grown at the same rate over the same period, Australia would now be home to well over 200 billion people. Yes, <u>billion</u>. That is ten thousand times more than the current population, in barely thirty years. Unsurprisingly, however, neither revenues nor profits have grown anything like as rapidly, as economies of scale, technological innovation and competition drive down the cost year by year.

The real challenge that results from this for companies is the timescales over which they invest and expect success. Fortunately, most corporations have evolved from relying on simple metrics such as payback periods, which typically place a very high emphasis on the very near term. Nevertheless, discounted cash flow valuations still typically place at least half of the emphasis on the first ten years of ownership. This is a direct result of the discount rates used, all lovingly calculated using the capital asset pricing model, and typically at least 10% to 15% a year around the world. In other words, investors are expecting to achieve a return on their investment of at least 10% to 15% a year for the long term.

This is particularly for new, higher growth businesses, where discount rates as high as 25% to 35% or more may be used. In other words, typically businesses with higher growth potential will be perceived as riskier, and less emphasis will be placed on the long term. At 35%, over two thirds of the weighting is placed on just the first four years of ownership. Only 5% of the value lies after year ten, and more or less none after year 20. Apple is, of course, over thirty years old already, and virtually all the value was created after its twentieth birthday.

This illustrates just how blunt an instrument conventional discounted cash flow models are in investigating value in potentially very high growth companies. Critically, this approach tends to use a base case and a few upside and downside scenarios, and blurs the assessment of likely returns with measures of risk, with both factored together in determining the discount rate to be applied. This makes it all too easy to overlook scenarios in which dramatic amounts of value will be created or destroyed. If these concepts don't resonate with you, then ask yourself this question. What would make you change your mind? What case studies would you want to see that demonstrated that the conventional approach to using discounted cash flow valuations led to the wrong decisions being made, more risk and less profit?

THE LONG TERM STARTS TOMORROW (PART 1)

The Long Term Starts Tomorrow has three broad themes. The first is that the methodologies that underpin a substantial amount of decision-making are fundamentally flawed. There is good evidence of this all around us in the corporate success stories and disasters of the last twenty years. Slavish trust in these approaches increases risk and destroys value. Meanwhile, business leaders everywhere face an increasingly unpredictable world, where significant changes in technologies and business conditions are occurring more and more frequently.

How do we deal with this? The first part of this book aims to prompt you to think about the world in new ways that will give you a much more robust way of grappling with the uncertainties that face businesses and Governments every day:

- "The two percent challenge" (chapter 2) highlights the importance of longer term thinking and offers a simple test to identify situations where the right longer term perspective will create real value and where the strategy that seems "right" in the short term may add to next year's profits but destroy a substantial amount of value in just a few years; and

- "Burn the base case: welcoming complexity" (chapter 3) looks at uncertainty in a way that allows you to embrace widely divergent outcomes and risk, rather than blending them in to a base case scenario that entirely obscures real opportunities for value creation and destruction. How can you escape arbitrary upside and downside scenarios and grapple properly with the much wider range of outcomes that occur in real life?

This analysis may be uncomfortable for some and I warmly welcome challenges to the thinking. A focus on the short term is a natural, animal instinct so it is no surprise that voters and shareholders are attracted more by the glitter of short term gain and worry less about the longer term impacts. In doing so, however, the evidence shows that they are missing massive opportunities.

But better analysis is not the only challenge and improved economic terms are not the only priority. The second broad theme is that better decision-making will also make for more sustainable organisations and will also drive better overall economic and social outcomes over the longer term too. Quite simply, there will be more profit, more value and less risk, from taking a longer term approach. Business models, corporate complacency and deeply ingrained thinking all act to limit opportunities and constrain growth. Awareness of these constraints is critical for organisations to be able to free themselves from the shackles of habit and linear thinking:

- "Casting off the chains of the free market" (chapter 4) explores how business models, industry structures and vested interests create formidable barriers to innovation and the realisation of growth strategies;

- "The supremacy gene – fighting the enemy within" (chapter 5) sounds a cautionary note regarding the perils of success itself, exploring how organisations afflicted with the supremacy gene choose paths of inevitable decline and fall, secure in the innate self belief that they are absolute masters of their own destiny;

- "The energy revolution – exploring a new growth paradigm" (chapter 6) examines how pre-conceptions are often allowed to influence or even determine strategic decisions, by framing a set of challenges in a manner that diverts attention from the real opportunities and risks.

Understanding these challenges and having some new tools to tackle them is critically important. What matters even more is making and implementing the decisions that will drive real change. So the third broad theme relates to how we can best harness this thinking to imagine new futures, judging our success by measures that are more likely to drive profitable growth over the medium to long term, not just the next few years:

- "An obituary for financial rationalism" (chapter 7) provides a brief look back over the evolution of intellectual and corporate thinking over the post war period, reflecting on its successes and drawing out the fundamental flaws that must be addressed if organisations are to make better decisions and avoid repeating the disasters of recent decades;

- "You've escaped, so don't look back!" (chapter 8) highlights the perils of assuming that methodologies and conceptual thinking that worked well in the past will continue to work in the present, let alone the future. Great courage will be required to adapt to a world where doing things differently may be safer than sticking with what is familiar, and organisations will have to work hard to introduce a bias for change into their cultures; and

- "Never mind the strategy, where are we going?" (chapter 9) provides a simple, powerful framework for guiding organisations through change, whether this is strategic, structural, operational or cultural in nature.

The epilogue to this book (chapter 10) is in part a thank you to Jorgen Randers, who inspired this book through his personal warmth, thoughtful conversation and pragmatism in the face of the world's exceptionally slow response to the concepts of system limits on growth. The various ideas in this book were sparked by a series of discussions in Sydney, Australia. More than anything, the conversations set me thinking about how, with all the advances in management theory, and financial analysis, and information and communications could the world economy have got so rapidly to such a dark place. More importantly, how could we think differently about these challenges and find ways to make decisions that would prove more robust and sustainable over the medium to long term.

Importantly, this is also a call to action. The cautionary tale of the frog sitting in a pot of cool water on the stove is well known. Jorgen's own frog represents his belief that the market liberalist world view will continue to drive human decision-making. We will be afraid to embrace uncertainty and until we do we will remain handicapped by our collective propensity to let short-term considerations dominate our thinking at the considerable expense of better long term outcomes.

"Saving Jorgen's frog" is designed to show that almost any kind of change can be achieved with a mixture of courage, the right mindset and the right friends.

2. The Two Percent challenge

SHORT TERM GAIN, LONG TERM PAIN

The business world is relentlessly focussed on results and outcomes, but how often do you think about what these words really mean? For many in the financial community around the world, these terms have a very immediate meaning, driven by corporate reporting cycles, not to mention personal financial rewards and promotions. Long term strategy rarely looks more than five years into the future, and this seems justified given fickle consumer desires and the pace of change of so many aspects of business life.

But – and this is a big but – for nearly all businesses, and especially for the most successful ones, nearly all the shareholder value will be made over the longer term, not just the next few years. So if your decision-making tools favour short term returns, you may well miss the best opportunities.

Despite this, the 1990s conversion to the religion of discounted cash flow valuations has driven an obsession with short term profitability that I think borders on the insane. In the last decade, there are numerous examples of businesses whose valuations have changed markedly as a result of pursing strategies that generated attractive short term returns, but destroyed a substantial shareholder value remarkably quickly. Nokia's relentless obsession with candy bar phones, in favour of flat touch screen designs, is just one example to which I return later.

Meanwhile the opposite is also true. The greatest value creation has come from companies that eschewed near term profits – indeed in some cases generated no revenue at all – in favour of building consumer relationship that would become valuable over the medium to long term. Each of Google, Yahoo, Facebook, Twitter, not to mention many other internet companies, have built businesses of substantial value out of an initial customer proposition that generated no revenue at all.

Of course in between are those for whom the jury is still out, and we will return to some of them later. In the meantime, remember that many of the people who call on you day by day to generate short term results will be gone in five or ten years time. Hopefully your company will remain, stronger than ever, helped by short term decisions that have stood the test of time.

The investment banking industry itself, theoretically the bastion of wise investing and financially sophisticated decision-making, provides a perfect example of the dramatic changes of fortune that come from choices that turned out to be unwise. Recent years have seen the demise of a number of great names. Some failed outright, others were shepherded into the arms of commercial bank suitors, and virtually all the rest had to be bailed out by Governments around the world. These were nearly all multi-billion dollar companies with 50 to 100 years of tremendous successes behind them. Virtually all of them had achieved this success using their employees' own capital, at a time when these organisations were privately-owned companies or partnerships.

Before them, most of the world's great merchant banks had disappeared in the 1990s, unable to find a way to compete effectively against much younger, more aggressive competitors from the United States and copy cats from Continental Europe. Kleinwort Benson was acquired by Dresdner Bank, SG Warburg by UBS, Schroders by Citigroup, Morgan Grenfell by Deutsche Bank and Flemings by JP Morgan. Meanwhile Barings failed, brought down by a total breakdown of basic controls around derivatives trading, and was acquired by ING from the administrators. The Barings name is now long since erased from the financial markets. From a peer group that had once been as powerful as Europe's leading nations, only Rothschild remains.

Much has been written on the corporate journeys of each of these businesses. A common theme to many of the stories has been a focus on near term opportunism and profit, not to mention personal empire-building on the part of key executives and the obsession with annual bonus payments. Remember, this is an industry sector that has depended first and foremost on reputation since the formation of the first merchant bank, Barings, in 1762. Thus one question is critical to keep in mind as you read. Which organisations have truly added to their reputation amongst their customers, and the esteem in which they are held by society in general, over the last decade?

My point is not to examine the rights and wrongs of the world's financial system here. Rather it is simply to highlight how the pursuit and delivery of short term bonuses and record profitability was so closely aligned in time and space with a dramatic collapse in value. At its peak in 2007, the combined market value of the world's five leading US investment banks was $421 billion. One year later, it had fallen by 87% to just $56bn. A further five years on, investment bank share prices still remain well below their peaks, despite a dramatic recovery in world equity markets. And other once-illustrious names, such as Lehman Brothers, have been consigned to the graveyard that lies so fittingly at one end of Wall Street.

In the corporate world too, pursuit of profit and shareholder value over the short term has often turned surprisingly rapidly to financial ruin. In some cases, the cause has been outright fraud (eg Enron) or reputational damage (Arthur Andersen). In others, strategic myopia, personal ambition and sheer greed have played a strong role. Much more worrying than these extreme examples are the many occasions when organisations decide that it is simply "too risky" to innovate or follow a new pathway, and instead seek to focus on their existing strengths. Nokia's failure to dominate smart phones in the way that it had led the world with 2G/GSM handsets is a case in point.

In short, it is all too easy for the ordinary business executive to have little intuitive feel for the importance of decadal long trends, let alone a view of centuries. Indeed, even the mention of a twenty year time horizon – let alone a century – would seem to be something much better suited to a history lecture than a business text. With this in mind, think about basic infrastructure, such as roads, railways and communications networks. Much of the infrastructure on which European nations depend was built in the 19th century or early 20th century. Around the world, the comment is often heard "we couldn't afford it now as labour was so cheap then". In many cases, the truth is that the economic and financial returns were only realised over many decades – these projects would never have stood the supposedly rigorous test of modern day financial analysis. In other words the economic prosperity enjoyed by some of the world's leading nations rests on investments made many decades ago. This is well outside the normal time horizons considered in business.

WOULD YOU DISCOUNT YOUR FAMILY?

So, how did organisations ever become so obsessed with the near term? Part of this is a result, of course, of culture. But let's start with the main financial tool that has driven business decision-making for the last twenty years, the discounted cash flow valuation. This approach is based on the principal that, for any investment, you need to see an adequate return on your money, allowing for the effects of time. In addition, you need to build in a suitable premium for risk. Typically companies will require a rate of return of at least 10% to 12% a year in the developed world, and will often target annual returns of 15% or more. If you are not familiar with discounted cash flow techniques, you will probably have little appreciation for just how strongly skewed to the very near term these approaches are. But the basic concept probably sounds logical to you.

To bring all this to life, think about what would happen if you applied the theories of discounting to the people around you. Not literally, of course, but in terms of the relative importance you place on different parts of their lives. How much weight would you instinctively place on things that are important for your children – or grandchildren – compared to the time or money you might spend on yourself over the next few years?

First, ask yourself this question. When were your grandparents' grandparents born? For me, the answer is around 1850. Your own grandparents will doubtless remember some of their stories, of a life before the motor car, or domestic electric power, or even flushing toilets.

Then ask yourself, when will your grandchildren's grandchildren live to? These individuals – voters, shareholders, consumers – will hear your own stories second hand, from your grandchildren. These people are relatively close family members, and intuitively we should care about them. Even if life expectancy does not increase beyond a 100 years, for those with younger children the date is close to 2200. This is nearly two hundred years from today, and highlights how even the lives of relatively close family members will span some 350 years.

Think about how much has already happened within this time frame. Since 1850, there have been significant revolutions in energy (electricity, power stations, nuclear power), transport (the motor car), long distance telecommunications (radio and telephones), the mass media (radio and television), long distance travel (air travel), automation (through the use of IT), mobile communication (first and second generation mobile phones) and most recently mobile data via 3G and 4G networks. There have also been dramatic innovations in healthcare, including antibiotics, organ replacement, nearly all drugs currently in use today, medical imaging and diagnostics and many others. This is far from a complete list – the point is simply to illustrate how dramatic the changes have been within just a few generations.

Going back to our extended family, between them, these nine generations will span most of four centuries. For nearly all of us, the first two generations will already have passed away. Of the remaining seven, however, around two thirds are as yet unborn.

So, when we are making decisions in business, or Government or society more generally, how much weight should we give each of these seven generations? This may be a deep, existential question, but the financial rigour of discounting can easily be applied, as it is so often in the business world. If you think this is a horrifying concept, then you must read on. If you don't, then just follow the maths.

First of all, let's just think about one person from each generation that is still living or unborn, from your perspective. So there are seven people in all – one grandparent, a parent, you, one child, a grandchild, a great grandchild and a great great grandchild. With some typical assumptions for longevity, these people will between them live for a total of just under 400 person years, spread between now and the year 2,200.

For a 45 year old representative of generation X, your own life would contribute around 10% of the total, as would the combined lives of your parents and grandparents. The subsequent four generations would account for roughly 20% each, ie a total of 80%. So if each person's life was treated equally, there would be a significant emphasis on the longer term.

What would happen if you placed a reducing emphasis on future years using the "rigour" of discounting? Let's use a discount rate of 15%, a common target for many businesses over the last twenty years. If you've never worshipped at the altar of Modigliani and Miller, then just be aware that this approach would use a unit value of 1 for the first year, $1/(1+0.15)$ or about 0.86 for the second year, $0.86/(1+0.15)$ ie roughly 0.75 for the third year etc.

Out of the four hundred person years we mentioned above, how many years are there in net present value terms?

Just 22.6! Think for a moment about the implications of this. Effectively the whole of the rest of time – not to mention the generations that live in those future years – gets condensed into just 22.6 years.

So whose life is important on this metric? Before you snap the pages shut in horror, remember that this is precisely the calculation that is being used every minute of every day around the world to make business and Government decisions.

Discounting places a heavy emphasis on the nearer years, so you won't be surprised to know that great grandchildren and great great grandchildren don't get a look-in. They are lost in the rounding. Effectively, if you are born after 2075, you just don't matter. Of course, when your own grand-parents were born, you were yourself one of these valueless descendants, a character in a year more than 60 years from today that simply "has no value".

Meanwhile even the grandchild only accounts for 1% of the total, or about nine weeks out of the 22.6 years. Of course, if your grandchildren are already alive, they will rank a little better, but not much.

Of the remaining 99%, there are roughly equal periods for you and your children – about six and a half years each, or a bit less than a third of the total. There are 5½ years for your parents and just 3.4 for your grandparents. As a result, virtually all the emphasis is placed on current generations. In fact over 80% of the "value" of these lives is attributed to just the next ten years.

These figures should be shocking – surely there must be few people who would completely ignore even the teenage years of a newborn child when making decisions about their family's future? But this is precisely the implication of discounted cash flows – a decision-making tool that is in use every day.

So where's the flaw?

The critical flaw is that, for businesses that grow even modestly, the large majority of profit, even using the discounting methodology, lies relatively far in the future. Indeed, the higher growth the company, the further in the future most of the value lies. Neither Google nor Facebook made any profit in their first five years of operation. For example, for a company that projected to grow at 52% a year (the same rate achieved by Google since its IPO), over half the total projected *profit* would be made in the last two years of a ten year time horizon. Even after discounting at 15%, the figure is still 46%.

And of course the capital value of the business at the end of ten years would be immense. In Google's case, it is now valued at 12x current year profits. If you add in the capital value to the example above, then 87% of the overall value lies in the final year, even in net present value terms. So, if you are looking for high growth, high value opportunities, the near to medium term doesn't really matter at all. And if you rely on the perceived rigour of discounted cash flow valuations, you will probably never find these opportunities.

Of course, most real world businesses don't grow at 52% a year. Indeed over the long term, very few businesses have managed to achieve compound growth in profits of more than 10% to 15%. Even the mighty Apple has only grown profits at a compound rate of 31% a year since its first million dollar profit of $5.1m in 1979, and at just 24% a year over the last twenty years.

Unsurprisingly, corporate decision-making typically places a strong emphasis on the near term. Discounted cash flow valuations and the cult of financial rationalism has allowed financial arguments to appear highly rigorous and undermine leaders seeking to deliver longer term visions. All of this has, of course, been exacerbated by the very short term focus of investment markets and financial commentators, with Boards and management all too often sucked in to the negative vortex of quarterly reporting and knee jerk reactions to movements in the share price.

As a result, even where dramatic industrial change is relatively predictable, companies may "err on the side of caution" and adopt strategies that will work well in the near term. By implication, of course, these strategies may turn out to be much riskier over the longer term, but somehow there is a comfort in the status quo. Of course these risks inevitably come home to roost, very often much more quickly that the Board or management may have hoped, and CEOs and management teams are unceremoniously dumped from what is all too often their last executive role.

There are many examples of companies and other organisations making decisions that will affect the long term prospects and positioning of their company based solely on short term perspectives. Over the last decade, investors threw many tens of billions of dollars into private equity funds, lured by the promise of massive returns levered by record-breaking levels of debt. Motor manufacturers ignored the promise of emerging markets such as India, allowing Tata to acquire iconic brands such as Range Rover, Jaguar and Landrover, not to mention launching its own, highly innovative Tata Nano designed particularly for the needs of the emerging Indian mass market. The latter was driven by the vision of the Chairman, Ratan Tata, who wanted to give "the common man" – who is a well understood character in India – a vehicle that he or she could afford.

Ultimately, this short term focus is not surprising. Around the world, in most businesses remuneration structures typically to place a strong emphasis on quarterly or six monthly or yearly performance metrics, with very few employees incentivised based on performance over longer time periods. "Optimisation of efficiency" bred a culture whereby job security became a thing of the past, with employers free to hire and fire at will. Employees responded in kind, making decisions for themselves and for their companies that would stand the test of year end reporting, even if they proved disastrous within a year or two.

As an aside, it's interesting to consider briefly the decision-making cultures in privately-owned companies around the world, such as Germany's economic "Mittelstand" powerhouse. Often dismissed by men in sharp suits as "unsophisticated", there are plenty of family-owned businesses around the world that demonstrate clearly a much stronger focus on the long term. These companies are not obsessed with the number at the bottom of a 250,000 cell discounted cash flow model, nor are they interested in arguing the niceties of discount rates or "maximising the efficiency of the company's capital structure" (aka leveraging it to within an inch of its life – or death). What their Boards and management teams do care about is making decent profits in the near term, and leaving a strong and prosperous business behind for future generations. This is sustainability and long term value creation in action.

No-one ever got fired for hiring IBM

So who should be looking out for the company's longer term interests? Risk aversion – and in particular aversion to very near term risks in preference for accepting longer term risks – is a direct product of performance indicators, remuneration structures and culture. So this places a heavy onus on those who create those structures – essentially boards and senior management teams – to play a strong roll in balancing short-termism.

But how often does this happen in real life? All too many CEOs and their direct reports are under more or less daily pressure to deliver improved results and other targets, and Boards feel the watchful eye of external scrutiny with great sensitivity. All too often, when near term performance appears to flag, the Board will resort to a change of CEO. Average CEO tenure in countries such as the US and UK has averaged below four years in recent times, substantially shorter than typical Board tenure of around a decade (nine years in the case of the UK's Cadbury regime).

There would seem to be plenty of empirical evidence that this short-termism by Boards is itself ineffective – there seems to be little correlation between a Board's propensity to change CEOs frequently and positive share price performance. Indeed I suspect the reverse may be the case.

The irony, of course, of the above expression is that it relates to the choice of IBM for major hardware projects in the 1970s and 1980s – since then, of course, IBM has had to reposition its business dramatically towards services, in the face of a hardware proposition that was undermined by low cost, high quality competitors that reinvented the business model for manufacture and sale of PCs and low end servers.

And of course, there are many, many CEOs, senior executives and other staff members who did get fired for "having their head in the sand", or whose reputations were tarnished as peers and commentators wondered "Why didn't they see this coming?".

FLIRTING WITH PERMANENCY – INTRODUCING THE 2% CHALLENGE

Part of this came about because economies were growing at historically very high rates. Imagine, for a moment, if your economy wasn't growing at 4% or 5% a year in real terms? Economic growth was virtually non-existent prior to the 18th century. In fact, over most of the last 800 years, growth in major economies has averaged less than 2% a year, so this isn't that unusual. Indeed Japan's economy has grown less than 1% a year over the twenty years since 1992. And since the financial crisis in 2008, most of the largest Western economies have suffered significant setbacks.

How would you behave differently? If residential property prices were only going to increase by 12% over the next 20 years, would you still see property as the best place for the average person to put most of their wealth? Would you still want to retire at 60, and fund 25 to 35 years of retirement from your savings, if you were only generating a return of 3% or 4% a year in nominal terms? Would you start to think a bit harder about your own personal earnings profile over the longer term? What if you knew that you wouldn't be getting real pay increases either, at least not for the next decade or two?

This is how you would start to think in a world where change – at least in an economic growth and financial market return sense – was much lower. If you had a perfect crystal ball, and anticipated this change in environment, then you would start to use much lower discount rates. If risk also reduced, then discount rates would fall even further. And looking back in history, it was this perspective which allowed major pieces of infrastructure to be built, driven by the desire to realise opportunities over the longer term and not simply short term discounted cash flow forecasts.

As an aside, Lord Stern provoked extensive discussion and not a little criticism for his use of a discount rate of just 1.4% in his "Review on the Economics of Climate Change". His fundamental point was that any such review should not disregard the impact of the actions or inactions of today on future generations. But plenty of people have argued strongly the opposite case – that market discount rates should apply and, by implication, that we should essentially disregard anything that is more than 20 years or so in the future.

Let's return to discounting your family for a moment. With a discount rate of 2% (instead of 15%), instead of just thinking about 22.6 person years, we'd be up to around 127. You and your own children would still have a strong weighting, at 53%, but great grandchildren would still count for 10% and great great grandchildren for 5%. You would be placing much more weight on events further in the future, and you wouldn't be almost entirely focussed on the next ten years. I would hope that to most, if not all, readers, this would seem like a much more natural result, with consideration being given to generations that will be born within our children's lifetimes.

What is most important, however, is not the number of years, or even the weightings, but whether you would simply make different decisions as a result of taking a longer term view. This is a fundamentally important point.

If this change in discount rate, or increased weighting of the slightly longer term over the near term, leads to a different decision, then this is a powerful signal that you may need to rethink your priorities and your choices. This signal tells you that an inflexion point is approaching, and that there will come a time in the relatively near future when the priorities driving short term decisions will be replaced by a different paradigm. It is also an important reminder that the widely used tool of discounted cash flow valuations is not necessarily an effective one for identifying significant upside opportunities or avoiding major downside risks over the medium to long term.

DO YOU WANT TO PLAY RUSSIAN ROULETTE, CORPORATE STYLE?

But how can we adapt this thinking for use in the business world, where the reality of near term performance remains? We have already seen a powerful diagnostic tool – the 2% challenge. Simply re-run your valuation analysis using a much lower discount rate, and explore whether this would cause you to reach a different conclusion regarding any particular strategy or decision. The point is not to invest on such metrics, but rather to identify factors or decisions that will have a material bearing on the longer term success or failure of the organisation, even if the near term impacts are relatively small. This approach will flush out decisions that will eventually have to be made, or risks that will eventually have to be addressed, even if they are not made today.

Building on this, many organisations will be able to make small investments today that help to position the organisation for that eventual change. Indeed the costs of such early investment may be minimal, and the upside may be very great.

Obvious examples include major capital investments, which are simply "not economic" at the moment, as well as addressing the need to find profit to replace that generated by a successful, but declining, cash cow business. In a world that is changing ever more rapidly, other relevant examples include finding a way to compete effectively in a new, but rapidly growing, market niche as well as blue sky developments (the $100 billion hiding in your garage).

These decisions will often be linked to future inflexion points in a company's development. For Apple, it was the iPod and iPhone, both of which redefined the company, its products and how it was perceived, unlocking hundreds of billions of dollars of shareholder value. Other companies have achieved the same. In the 1980s,

Tesco was a drab second rate UK supermarket that was only your first choice if there was nowhere else to go. Over the space of the next decade, the company transformed itself into the UK's leading food retailer, not to mention a successful bank, the country's leading internet retailer and a top five retailer in books, toys, electrical equipment and home products. Once again, the critical early choices were made more or less a decade ahead of when the real value was unlocked.

If you can identify decisions of this nature, then you can also start to think about the risks associated with them. Importantly, this doesn't just mean the risks of pursuing such opportunities, but also the risk of not pursuing them. This is the corporate Russian roulette played out year by year at annual strategy retreats around the world. Longer term risks are discounted, and plenty of companies spin the barrel, hoping that by deferring investment and innovation, higher short term profits will be enough to get them through to next year's game. Then corporate executives pull the trigger and hope that the status quo can be maintained for a couple more years until their next promotion.

The successful blindly go on playing this game year after year, with no ill effects. The unlucky discover that a new competitor has marched in and redefined their industry, taken their best customers, and created new billion dollar profit streams that they simply cannot access themselves.

The 2% challenge gives you a simple methodology to apply that will highlight fundamental downside risks associated with inaction. Critically, you can start to ask how you can launch the requisite strategies or developments in a manner which minimises near term costs, but ensures that you are ready to move pro-actively when the market in question emerges from its infancy. It will also give you the opportunity to seek to shape the market in ways which best suit your own capabilities, market position and business model. In doing so, you must of course beware that attempting to mould the customer to fit your own desires may be profitable in the short term, but rarely creates businesses that are sustainable over the longer term.

3. Burn the base case: welcoming complexity

COULD YOUR WEAKEST COMPETITOR OUTGROW YOU 400x?

For nearly every organisation, one of the most critical challenges is uncertainty. The level of complexity faced by individuals, businesses and governments has increased dramatically over the last fifty years, arguably matched only by an accelerating rate of change in technology. In many industries, this has made it harder and harder to anticipate the nature and timing of revolutionary changes, increasing the perception that many more decisions are inherently highly risky.

The development of television provides a great illustration of these trends. From the first black and white broadcast (in the UK 1929), it took over 40 years until the US had an all colour TV season. It took another 30 years to begin the transition to high definition broadcasts, and this process remains under way around the world. The next generation of high definition TV, so-called 4K screens with double the resolution of "Full HD" TV will become the staple in 2014. Meanwhile "Super Hi Vision" technology, which offers 16x the resolution of current HD, has already been piloted at the London Olympics. It will launch commercially in 2020, 20 years after HD entered the mainstream.

Having once been multi-decadal in nature, these changes in mass TV technology are happening more and more quickly and the rate of consumer take-up is accelerating as affordability improves significantly year by year. Meanwhile, mobile device screens and technologies have evolved much more rapidly, with last year's leading edge technology already approaching ubiquitous deployment despite the best efforts of patent breach litigators around the world.

Looking forward, 4G mobile phone systems are rolling out globally, and the war for dominance in the sector is more intense than ever before. The battles are being played out not just on the device playing field (Apple, Samsung, Nokia, Blackberry, HTC and many others), but also amongst operating system providers (Apple, Google/Android, Blackberry and Microsoft). The size of the prize for combatants is enormous – at least $1 trillion of market value rests on the sale of devices and their associated operating systems alone. Reflecting the intensity of competition, the battles extend beyond technology innovation, design and marketing to some of the most complex, and most expensive, multi-jurisdictional litigations ever brought forward.

The key challenge for any competitor in this space – or indeed potential new entrants – is to be able to envision and describe likely market conditions and consumer preferences just a few years in the future. With product life-cycles continuing to reduce, this simply gets harder and harder year by year. Three years ago, Apple's iPhone reigned supreme. In 2013, the iOS operating system has a share of just 15% of new handset sales, only a fifth that of Android on 77%.

Despite the perceived advantages of incumbency, markets for technology products have in practice been incredibly dynamic. Each new television technology has seen new product leaders emerge. Do you even remember the brand of television you watched as a child? A decade ago, the screen of choice was almost certainly Sony. In more recent years it has been Samsung.

The same has been true in mobile devices. The original analogue handsets were dominated by Motorola's DynaTAC. The world's first GSM call was made by then Finnish Prime Minister Harri Holkeri on 2st July 1991 on a Nokia phone and Nokia network. Within a few years the company was the global leader in 2G handset sales. Apple revolutionised mobile devices with the iPhone – the world's first mass market smartphone, and was a clear market leader globally for the first 2G and 3G smartphones. With 4G services rolling out around the world, the Android operating system dominates, and Samsung has overtaken Apple as the mobile device of choice. And in all this Microsoft, which provided the operating system for nearly all personal computers for thirty years from the late 1970s, still has barely any market share in smartphones, by far the most common mobile computers of today. And even if you buy a phone with the Microsoft operating system, it still does not provide secure integration with office email in the way that Blackberry has delivered since 1998. I will watch with great interest to see what unfolds as Microsoft integrates the Nokia device business that it recently purchased.

Revolutionary changes in industry leadership are not confined to TVs and mobile phones. Apple created the tablet market almost overnight, after many much longer established companies had tried and failed. PC and laptop manufacturing market shares have changed dramatically over the last ten years. And there are many examples outside technology, with dramatic changes in global market share having been seen in the world airline sector, motor manufacturing, fashion brands, consumer dietary preferences and many more.

So the threat of technological development driving dramatic inflexion points in market position and profitability are very real.

Between March 1997 and March 2012, Apple's market value increased by a factor of around 400 times compared to Nokia, one of the most remarkable corporate value shifts of all time. No-frills airlines now have market values substantially higher than century-old aviation pioneers (many of whom have filed for bankruptcy over the years).

Importantly, many of these changes in fortune came about not because companies invested in the wrong project, but because they failed to invest in opportunities that would position them well as technology or markets evolved. Currently there is a significant shift of technology platforms and systems and associated services into the cloud. This offers the potential for much more wide-reaching implications than simply a change in the place where computations take place. Indeed in some segments there is every chance that today's powerful incumbents will be replaced by companies that were start-ups only a few years ago. Nowhere is the clearer than in the media sector, where once great national publishers have been usurped by the global power and reach of social media companies.

All too often, the best strategic options for the companies in question are obvious in retrospect. But beyond simply attributing this to 20:20 hindsight, forgiving managers and shareholders and moving on, it's important to think about whether, and more importantly, how better choices could have been made.

ABANDONING THE ANIMAL PREFERENCE FOR THE STATUS QUO

Animals have learned to trust their instincts – relying on following what has worked before as a lower risk option than trying something different. In the corporate world too, many strategies favour the status quo, in the belief that this helps to avoid risks and uncertainties. This "better the devil you know" mindset feels intuitively appealing, sticking with the risks that are familiar. But how often do companies actually take on risk – indeed exceptional risk – because they stick with the status quo and do not fully assess the medium or longer term risks of prospective industry change?

Very few companies run detailed forecasts that extend much beyond five years, and even high level strategic planning rarely addresses how the company may be positioned in ten years' time. Of course this approach worked very well in 1800, as the world was still changing very slowly. Even in 1950, the pace of change remained relatively modest, and so it was safe for organisations to pay relatively little attention to longer term planning. It's important to note, however, that this focus on the short term worked well precisely because change was slow. The longer term was still critically important to corporate value and it was simply that the near term was essentially a good guide to longer term outcomes. Corporate plans could be adjusted slowly – small shifts to the corporate steering wheel every three to five years – and the organisation could evolve its strategic position in a stately and low risk manner. And indeed, with business cultures at that time still delivering "job for life" employment security, individuals within an organisation were also incentivised to look out for the longer term health and success of their companies, which would eventually pay their pensions.

As an example, the world's oldest company, Japanese builder Kongo Gumi, survived for centuries under the guidance of 40 generations of family ownership. Even when it reached the end of its natural corporate life, it still took decades to die. It was only acquired in 2006 under severe financial distress. In contrast, in the last decade, a number of very well-known companies (such as Enron, Arthur Andersen, Lehman and Bear Sterns) have moved from global leadership positions to chapters in the history book in a matter of months or even weeks.

I see Boards and management teams grappling with this challenge time and time again in my role as a corporate advisor. It is a new challenge, arising from the dramatically greater rates of change with which businesses and Governments must deal. As one example, motor manufacturers were able to focus on a single propulsion technology (the internal combustion engine) for many decades, safe in the knowledge that it offered a fundamentally better solution that the alternatives. Over the last fifteen years, since the launch of the Toyota Prius in 1997, hybrids have begun to emerge, but they were in most regards simply a variant on a traditional fossil fuel car. In twelve short months, Tesla's Model S has changed the game completely, offering a vehicle that is fundamentally different from – and better than – the competition in many ways. So although ignoring electric vehicles for the last twenty years has proved a perfectly reasonable strategy, suddenly the rules of the game are changing – I will return to how a little later.

So, in a world where revolutionary technological or societal change is emerging in much shorter time frames, it is no longer safe to assume that the current five year plan will still be even modestly relevant by year six. Even with a five year plan that is updated every year, there is real risk that fundamental strategic repositioning or organisational design will be deferred too long, forcing the organisation to attempt dramatic business change too quickly and too late, when the pressure from a new competitor or changing market dynamics have really begun to bite.

In this environment, traditional financial projection models simply do not paint a realistic view of the range of outcomes that needs to be considered. Even if they make extensive use of "sensitivity tables" and "scenario analysis", very rarely do they really draw out in any meaningful way the likelihood that more extreme outcomes than shown in the scenarios will actually appear in real life. This is a fundamental flaw in the entire philosophy that underpins the financial evaluation of long term strategy, and goes a long way to explaining how such dramatic successes and failures can happen so quickly.

WHAT DO YOU DO WHEN THE AVERAGE NEVER HAPPENS?

There are many industries where forecasting realistic business outcomes involves much more than simply adding 10% to this year's revenues or profits. In the most extreme cases, the most likely profit outcomes are more or less binary year by year, ranging between significant gains and at least moderate losses.

Consider for a moment the prospects of Cubbie Station, one of the world's largest farms. Located near Dirranbandi and St George, in South West Queensland, Australia, the property covers some 93,000 hectares, making it considerably larger than the nation of Singapore. The property benefits from water licenses which allow a small percentage of the flow of three rivers in the Balonne region to be diverted into an enormous water storage facility. These rivers are part of the Murray Darling river system, which lies in a catchment area of over a million square kilometres, larger than France, Germany and Switzerland combined. The Murray River itself is over 2,500 km long. The terrain is relatively flat, meaning the river is slow moving, and floodwaters from storms in Queensland take over three months to flow to the lower reaches of the river. At full capacity – which can only be used in times of major flood – Cubbie can store 537,000 megalitres of water, enough to meet the entire water needs of London, UK, for over ten months. In its current configuration Cubbie is one of the largest cotton producers in the world, with capacity to grow 200km^2 of cotton.

But it doesn't always rain. Indeed, in recent history there have been periods as long as two years (September 1991 to August 1993) where Cubbie has been unable to extract any water at all from the rivers that flow past its storage facilities. This is because the terms of the water licenses are designed to ensure that a minimum level of environmental flow is maintained wherever possible, even in times of relatively prolonged drought. Indeed there have been periods as long as five years where there is no water in the dams at the time planting decisions need to be made. From September 1963 to September 1970, the estimated total flows were 8.7 GL. So in seven years Cubbie received less than the equivalent of just one year's median flow (9.8 GL).

The water records date back to the nineteenth century. From these you can see that about 30% of the time, the property has sufficient water to ensure full production. But 20% of the time, there is no production at all. In these years, Cubbie will make a loss, reflecting a basic level of operational cost needed to maintain the property even when there is no production. On top of these binary risks of production, you have to overlay the added complexity of highly volatile world cotton prices, not to mention significant variances year by year in the cost of other agricultural inputs such as fertilisers and vehicle fuel, as well as other climatic factors which effect cotton yields.

All of this adds up to a highly variable outcome in any one year, ranging between very substantial profits and material losses. So a base case forecast that represented average production would be incredibly misleading, as this scenario is exceptionally unlikely to emerge in real life. In short, the average never happens – and most years don't even come close.

Of course the ability to store over 500 giga-litres of water in what is probably the world's largest private water tank helps to ameliorate this risk. If the dams are full, roughly two years of production are guaranteed. Selling prices can be hedged via forward sales, and most input costs can be locked down quite tightly over a two year period. But simply valuing the property based on just two years of profits would ignore the impact of longer term profits and losses. Perhaps unsurprisingly, the history of Cubbie shows quite clearly that the property has generally been overvalued by purchasers when the dams are full, and undervalued when they are empty. So you need a way to assess the value of the property – and identify the optimal capital structure – which embraces this uncertainty.

100% WRONG: GUARANTEED!

Other industries have similar challenges. Whether you are operating in resources, or drug development, or technology innovation, your business will face key milestones that it simply must meet, or the company or project will fail. In these industries, base cases are simply meaningless.

In pharmaceutical development, for example, drugs progress from theoretical pharmacological activity assessment (typically derived through computer modelling), through chemical synthesis, to testing of efficacy and safety in a series of trials. Each stage costs significantly more to complete that the previous one, and hence the risks multiply dramatically at each step. Once the final hurdle is complete and the drug is cleared for marketing, there is then typically just a seven to twelve year window in which to leverage your position as the patent holder for the compound in question, before it moves off patent and is opened up to generic competition. Consider the example of Pharmaxis, which lost nearly 90% of its market value in the space of twelve months when US regulators rejected its application to release a cystic fibrosis drug called Bronchitol.

In resources, the key steps relate to obtaining information regarding the extent, quality and accessibility of the resource, with each new bore or pilot well adding critical new information to one or more of these measures. Unlike many industries, the resources sector has established a code which provides for a common approach to describing risks and assessing the extent and nature of resources, namely the JORC code. Even with this code, however, the range of outcomes from any particular project is exceptionally wide and expected value is very hard to assess.

In both of these examples, unexpected roadblocks often occur, and can lead to significant delays, typically accompanied by cost overruns. In addition, both have substantial development lead times and face the risk of competing projects beating them to full production. Significant regulatory uncertainty is another factor, as are the effects of environmental and consumer protection legislation. Meanwhile, in resources in particular, commodities prices remain highly volatile, meaning that actual prices achieved per tonne may vary substantially from the initial assumptions.

One common element between all these businesses is that each organisation's success or failure is decided by the outcomes of a series of decision gates. At each of these points, the outcome may be binary, in terms of success or failure, or it may vary across a wide range of possibilities in a more or less predictable manner.

For these businesses, it seems blindingly obvious that conventional financial models just won't work. A set of projections based on average volumes, or average prices, or average success rates bares absolutely no relationship to the real world. Worse, the average outcome on some metrics – such as for pharmaceuticals – is likely to be failure rather than success, as so few drugs make it through to full scale consumer release.

So what do you do when average is an entirely meaningless concept? This is the case with Cubbie Station, where the dynamics of weather patterns and substantial on-farm water storage mean that most years are either feast or famine, with virtually no "average" years. How can you reliably address the extent of variability inherent in projecting realistic future results? Will this make the project more risky, and your decision more complex, or can you do this in a way that reduces risk and adds value? I will return to this theme shortly, but first we should also consider the challenges of growth.

Long term growth, short term insanity

Just imagine that you were sitting round the table with Steve Jobs in 2004 talking about Project Purple and the value it would create? Even if you did believe it was possible to become the world's leading smart-phone maker, what costs would you assume along the way? How would you assess the risks created by years of upfront investment and an uncertain ramp up in sales? And even if you were exploring these possibilities, how would you build them into the financial models of the day other than as extreme scenarios? How would you weight them? Thousands of innovators and would-be entrepreneurs around the world have dreams this big, but the evidence of history is that very, very few people have ever created even a billion dollars of value from their innovations. So the degree of scepticism and caution on the part of investors is understandably high, and hardly any of the dreamers have the hundreds of millions or even billions of dollars required to develop and launch a global product.

Steve Jobs' "reality distortion field" has been widely described. Clearly his ability to suspend not only his own belief about what was possible, but also that of his colleagues and their teams was extraordinary. The Apple business was built on a tenacious commitment to delivering a consumer experience and meeting a real or future consumer need in the best possible way. Of course there had to be a level of cost awareness, as end products had to be profitable, but Apple's innovation was not a product of spreadsheets and cash flow forecasts.

The iPhone was unveiled on 9th January 2007 and that day Apple shares closed at $92.57, up 8.3% to what was an all time high. But how many analysts updated their forecasts that day and set a new long term price target of $600? This was achieved in barely five years, a growth rate pretty much unthinkable for a $100 billion company. And remember, this was been achieved through just a couple of products, with a minimal number of variants.

Just like in science, where the radical leaps forward in understanding tend to come from left field, the Jobs reality distortion field allowed innovation and creativity to flourish. In doing so, Apple created extraordinary value out of a shift in markets – and indeed through creating a new market in the form of tablet computers, albeit one that had long been discussed in technology circles.

Meanwhile, the typical processing power of a computer chip has increased at a rate of something like 30% to 35% a year, more or less in line with long term growth in demand for internet bandwidth since 1980. The compounding effects of this are mesmerising and feel very disconnected from the real world. Nevertheless they have allowed dramatic technological innovation in areas such as mobile communications.

With this in mind, it is perhaps no surprise that technological evolution is progressing at a rate that is harder and harder to assess using traditional financial tools. For example, Google achieved a growth rate of 52% a year in profits between 2004 and 2010. Facebook's recent IPO assumed that it too would achieve a similar rate of growth over the decade following its own IPO, notwithstanding competition from companies such as Google.

But this kind of growth is far from the norm, and indeed is more or less mathematically impossible to achieve over anything other than very short time periods.

THE LIMITS TO (COMPOUND) GROWTH

In 1970, the Club of Rome published a study conducted on their behalf by researchers from MIT which examined the physical constraints on the world's growth, as defined by a series of systems (eg the amount of fish that can sustainably be taken from the world's oceans). I'll return to this seminal book "Limits to Growth" later, and for the present comment on analogous concepts in the business world.

Think about the long term impact of growth rates for a moment. Despite the corporate world's focus on rates of return of 10% to 15% or more, most of us live in a world where we are used to very low growth rates. Population in the West has typically grown at rather less than 1% a year. In fact, since the year 1400, the world's population grew at about 0.5% a year. At this rate, over a century, population would increase by about 65%.

Meanwhile, Western economies have grown at between 1.5% and 3% a year in real terms since the Second World War. These growth rates are equivalent to GDP doubling in around 23 to 45 years – almost imperceptible change to most people. But as growth rates increase, the effects multiply – Nigeria's population has grown at about 2.5% per year since 1960, and has quadrupled in that time, creating a rapidly growing burden on a country that is ill placed to support its own population.

Since the Second World War, investors have grown used to total returns on investment of the order of 7% to 8% annually. This equates to values doubling in just eight to ten years.

In very broad terms, most companies use a target rate of return on equity of between 12% and 15%. We have come to regard these figures as sounding deceptively modest. But the truth is, with a compound growth rate of 15%, value would triple in just a decade. Over a century, the value would increase by a factor of well over a million. With population growth of not much more than 1%, this would represent a one hundred thousand fold increase in total profits per head of global population, implying dramatic changes in wealth and standard of living.

Meanwhile, private equity investors often target rates of return of 20% a year or more. Over a hundred years, this would result in growth by a factor of nearly 100 million. If the world's population had grown this fast since 1945, the population would now be 485 trillion people. This is equivalent to a little more than three people for every square metre of the earth's surface, or about ten for every square metre of land. You wouldn't have room to sit down.

So if you project double digit growth rates for more than a few years at a time, the results are unlikely to be achievable for long unless you start from an extremely low base. For example, if you assume compound growth rates for corporate profits of even 10% a year for the long term, you rapidly reach projected economic outcomes that are absurd. The lesson here is critical – you simply cannot assume that 10% growth is a reasonable benchmark for the long term. But there will still be companies – even quite large companies – that do still manage periods of dramatically higher growth and share price appreciation over shorter time scales.

Long term value in a short term world

So here is the conundrum: how do you locate true long term value in a short term world, where the future is less and less predictable, and long term growth rates are likely be well below 10% a year? And for Governments, how can you justify investment in major infrastructure, when the true benefits may only emerge several decades in the future?

Making the right long term choice is especially challenging where there is potential for dramatic changes from the status quo over the near to medium term. Meanwhile, with growth rates in some niche segments running above 15%, even in the relatively short term, revolutionary changes in scale relative to peers can be achieved in the matter of a few years. As a reminder, the iPhone went on sale on 29th June 2007, barely five years ago, and now has a share of smart phone sales of around 15%. Google launched Android in 2008 and in just four years has built a dominant position with a market share of 75%. And the iPad was launched in 2010, creating its own category in which Apple still has a roughly 50% market share. Over the same time, Microsoft's Internet Explorer has seen its market share decline from a peak of over 90% to around 30%.

Even for relatively stable business, relatively small changes in key measures such as turnover frequently mask a much more dynamic underlying business. As an example, a mortgage bank's balance sheet may grow at around 10% a year. But this net change will be the product of redemptions and repayments of as much as 30% of all loans a year. So new lending would have to run at 40% a year to achieve a much smaller net growth figure. As a result, a modest reduction in new business levels will lead to a much more rapid decline in growth. For a motor manufacturer, modest changes in overall market share may mask much more significant shifts in individual segments. Of course over the space of a few years, these small changes eventually start to bite, leading to accelerating decline.

A huge amount of corporate decision-making is based on some form of financial analysis. This may be as simple as payback periods or return on investment, or it may be based on "a more sophisticated approach" such as discounted cash flow valuations. The basic problem with all of these techniques is that they rely very heavily on some type of projection of future performance and profitability. In other words, someone produces a set of forecasts for the business concerned. With luck, the forecasts are based on a level of track record in the sector concerned, to help ensure that the assumptions used have some sort of connection with historical performance. Indeed preferably the forecasts will be shown next to at least five years of history. In most cases, the investigation of potential future profitability will include some kind of sensitivity analysis.

All this sounds terribly logical. And in some segments, it can work perfectly well, often for quite long periods of time. "Business as usual" developments move at a pace that is often surprisingly slow. Believe it or not, Australia's largest department store retailers only began to explore online retailing seriously in 2012. Their lack of proper online presence would have been surprising to a US or UK consumer a decade ago. Nevertheless, over the intervening decade, the Australian market has changed only slowly.

CHANGE IS SLOW, BUT REVOLUTIONS HAPPEN OVERNIGHT

But revolutionary businesses and business models can transition from start-up hopeful to market leadership – in terms of opinions and consumer desires – more or less overnight. And this is where the real challenge lies in setting a strategy for your organisation that will stand the test of time. How can you anticipate these changes and the associated risks, and build them into your strategic thinking and financial analysis?

Hundreds of business text books describe methodologies for thinking about the longer term. Although each has its merit, none of the approaches commonly adopted in the business world provide robust and reliable ways to grapple with the financial implications of real uncertainty. This is particularly unhelpful for corporate decision-making, as long term strategic repositioning typically requires substantial capital investment at an early stage. At best, most businesses attempt to address complexity by considering a number of scenarios. The fundamental flaw in this approach is that it typically relies on linear thinking, projecting the market shares and performance of today's business into the future.

Between today and the year 2030, several transformational developments in technology will occur that will completely reshape the world in which we live. They are particularly likely in the fields of energy, computing and healthcare. Most will appear logical, particularly with hindsight. But others are likely to be in fields that are unthinkable even today. These revolutionary changes will create winners and losers, and the speed at which losers move from market leader to the corporate mortuary will be faster than ever.

To address these challenges, our firm has pioneered the development of a number of innovative techniques that bring together traditional discounted cash flow valuations with the rigorous assessment of risk distributions and uncertainty to provide a much more realistic simulation of the range of outcomes that is likely as any company develops over the medium to long term. Of course "likely" means "possible", with the more extreme positive and negative scenarios represented in statistically appropriate ways.

If this sounds like rocket science, it is – we use techniques honed in astrophysics to bring insight and clarity to otherwise impenetrable decisions. The academic thinking and technical details behind this approach go well beyond the scope of this book. They are, of course, well known to research scientists and around the world, and are deployed in quant trading desks in the world's financial centres every minute of every day. But they are hardly ever used in strategic planning and corporate financial analysis – once again, an industry has stuck with the status quo assuming that this choice is safer than to "Think Different!" (thank you Steve Jobs).

These techniques offer an excellent solution to a twenty year old problem. From very early in my investment banking career, I realised that any worthwhile financial model needed to have *a relatively small set of input assumptions*. The reason for this was very simple – if changes made to individual assumptions had no material impact on the overall value, then they were irrelevant.

There was no point modelling individual audit fees on each of twelve subsidiaries of a mid-sized hydro-electricity business, although believe it or not I've seen this done before. In other words, each control on the dial needed to have an impact otherwise it was nothing more than a distraction. Grouping sets of assumptions together into scenarios is one solution, but all too often these combinations are entirely arbitrary. Despite this consideration, you also need to ensure that the inputs are granular enough and that the modelling logic is precise enough to ensure that your financial model properly emulates the operation and performance of the underlying business (this is why I strongly advocate building every model from scratch and tip my hat to Henry Ford as I do so). So I concluded that simplification must not come at the expense of realism.

The alternative approach is to establish a range of assumptions for each input where there is material uncertainty. This can be as sophisticated as developing an appropriate probability distribution for each input. Using Monte Carlo simulations, you can then combine these in a statistically robust manner to identify distributions of outcomes that provide enormously greater insight into financial performance and valuation, not to mention the associated financial risks. If the analysis is done the right way, you will not be caught out by an unexpected "perfect storm" ever again.

Whilst this sounds a little complex, the outputs are a delight to discuss, as they connect very directly with real world events. As a result, they resonate much more strongly with business leaders and their teams than tables of -10%, -5%, 0, +5%, +10% sensitivities.

And critically, this approach avoids arbitrary sensitivity scales. Remember, if Apollo 11 had been 5% out, we would never have heard Neil Armstrong's famous words.

EMBRACING RISK AND WELCOMING UNCERTAINTY

The key here for any business or organisation is to embrace uncertainty in all its forms. Welcome uncertainty into your CEO's office and Boardroom, and find ways to assess, as reliably as possible, the extent and range of probabilities related to any particular risk. Think also about the key decision markers along the way, and what distribution of outcomes is logical at each of these points in time. Then find someone who can combine all these factors in a robust and meaningful way, to build you a new world, NOUVEAU™ cash flow analysis so that you understand the range of valuation outcomes that is to be expected, and where the really key trigger points are along your development path.

With the right approach, in most cases you will find that engaging with these uncertainties will allow you to exclude the worst theoretically possible outcomes, because there will be practical ways to mitigate the most significant downside risks. The other side of this critically important coin is that you arc also likely to find that there is value hidden in your company that runs the risk of never being unlocked, unless the right strategy is chosen.

If you have the courage to follow this path, you will find opportunities to create significant new value that can be realised much more rapidly than you might ever have thought was possible. This is the gateway to long term success. That's why I remind myself every day that the long term starts tomorrow - indeed it really starts now, so work out where you're going to go, pack your bags, have a good night's sleep, and start the journey when you wake.

4. Casting off the chains of the free market

IF THE FREE MARKET IS SO EFFICIENT, WHY DOESN'T IT WORK?

Around 70,000 commercial ships ply the oceans daily, transporting 90% of the world's goods from where they are mined, grown or made to where they are needed. This includes bulk carriers for resources and commodities, container vessels and oil tankers, as well as leisure craft such as cruise liners.

Shipping is the most energy efficient form of transport, but because its use is so widespread, the industry consumes some $100 billion of fuel a year, creating more emissions than countries such as Germany, Canada and the UK.

Let's forget the emissions for a moment. Imagine that you could just cut the fuel bill by as much as three quarters. This isn't just a hypothetical example. The International Maritime Organization highlighted in its recent study that improvements of up to 75% fuel efficiency were potentially achievable, through a range of current clean technologies and design elements for both new and existing ships. These include energy recovery (waste heat recovery from engines), hull optimisation, air lubrication, improved engines, use of wind power and the latest in rudders, hull coatings, and propeller technology.

This would save the industry around $70 billion a year, creating around $1.4 trillion in total value if you look at the savings as an annuity. That's roughly as much value as the entire capitalisation of all the companies listed on the Australian stock exchange. Surely this would be attractive?

"Ah, but what about the capital costs?", I hear you say. So imagine if part of the saving could be achieved by a new type of antifouling for commercial ships, which reduced friction as vessels moved through the water. This would, in turn, reduce fuel bills by as much as 15% to 20%. Imagine the payback period on this investment was around nine months, compared to the typical life of antifouling of up to five years for deep sea shipping. In a world where there is increasing pressure on the shipping industry from many sources, and where fuel costs have increased dramatically, such investment would seem logical. And there would be significant reductions in the carbon emissions from the world's shipping fleet.

Although this technology is well established, until recently it had not been deployed in any meaningful way. The practical obstacle is that the companies that own the ships (and hence paint their hulls) are not responsible for paying the fuel bills. Fuel bills are paid by the shippers who charter the boats in question. So it is industry structure, which has separated who pays the fuel bill from who might invest to make the ship fuel-efficient, that acts as an impermeable barrier to a systemic improvement that would benefit all parties. Manufacturers would benefit as their transport costs would be reduced (fuel costs are a significant element of overall costs). Consumers would benefit, as goods would be cheaper. And shipping companies would benefit through increased overall trade, and an improved return on their investment in their ships.

THE WHITE GOODS CONUNDRUM

The failures of the world's shipping industry are an example of the white goods conundrum from the 1980s and 1990s. For many years, domestic appliances such as refrigerators and washing machines have been significant consumers of both electricity and water. In countries where these basic necessities have been plentiful and cheap, power and water efficiency were not a major concern. Of course there would have been environmental benefits if manufacturers had invested in designing their appliances to use less power and water. But this could have added significant cost, without necessarily resulting in any material increase in the selling price that could be achieved, as consumers were not focussed on these capabilities. Meanwhile the benefits of reduced water and power bills would flow to the consumer and not the manufacturers.

Manufacturers could, of course, simply advertise that their machines were more energy or water efficient than others, but would consumers believe them? Would consumers even worry about these factors, and what might just be a few dollars a month on their energy bills, when they were buying a $500 or $1,000 or $2,000 washing machine?

What was needed was an industry wide scheme – one which achieved the joint purpose of raising awareness of the issues and the opportunity, as well as providing reliable, like for like benchmarking between different appliances and different manufacturers. We are all now familiar with the energy and water efficiency labelling schemes for washing machines and dishwashers. Ultimately, this is thanks to a 1992 initiative by the European Union, which legislated a mandatory point of sale labelling scheme, which initially rated refrigerators on a scale from A to G. Since then, new grades have been introduced, to reflect advances in technology, with the most energy efficient A+++ models being 60% more efficient than the best appliances just 15 years earlier.

And here is a critical point. Simply creating a meaningful discussion around energy efficiency, and giving consumers a rating system and a language to use that is easier than kilowatt hours has focussed attention on the opportunity of energy efficiency. Who in their right mind would buy a category G refrigerator, which used nearly ten times as much power as the most efficient alternative?

The answer for shipping is exactly the same. Commercial ships need a simple A to G rating system, so that when you book a Panamax or Capesize vessel to ship coal to your power stations, you can reliably choose a ship that will reduce your fuel bill, whoever the owner and wherever it is registered.

The good news is that you can do this today. Ironically, despite the obvious commercial interests of end users and the shipping industry itself in seeing this labelling scheme realised, it has taken the action of a not for profit body motivated by environmental concerns to bring it to life. Shippingefficiency.org, an initiative of Carbon War Room (founded by global entrepreneurs such as Richard Branson), provides energy efficiency ratings for some 60,000 ships worldwide, supported by industry partners such as Maersk Lines. Ultimately this is a strong argument in favour of ensuring that countries introduce strong policy infrastructure to shape their economies in ways that counter hard-wired market failures of this type.

HAVE YOU BUILT BARRIERS TO SUCCESS INTO YOUR BUSINESS?

The examples of fridges and ships above provide a great illustration of how an entirely logical industry structure and the associated business models can create significant barriers to improving efficiency and profitability. It is entirely logical that consumers pay their own power bills for the fridges they have plugged in at home – as the amount of power used will be depend more on how the consumer users the fridge than on its design and efficiency per se.

Nevertheless, without a reliable third party energy efficiency labelling scheme, this approach mitigates against the design of power-efficient fridges as it is hard for consumers to judge the impact of this efficiency themselves.

So have you built barriers to success into the structure of your own organisation, whether consciously or unconsciously? Every organisation should find a way to get an honest, impartial answer to this question regularly, mindful of the changing environment in which it is operating. These barriers to success can apply to individual companies, or even whole industries. I am not talking about the modest organisational challenges that led to the endless round of reshaping that keeps management consulting firms in business. Rather I'm thinking about much more profound barriers to success.

Large and medium sized organisations divide their businesses up into divisions and business units and departments, each focussing on different customer types, or industry segments, or parts of the value chain. These are then supported by shared services functions that leverage the group's strengths to optimise the cost efficiency with which common tasks or functions are performed across the group, as well as central/head office functions.

This structure separates capabilities, processes and decision-making into a series of independent compartments, which are simpler to understand and easier to manage. Inevitably, as management seeks metrics by which to manage and incentivise individual teams, internal charging structures and transfer pricing arrangements are put in place. Typically these are designed, at least at a point in time, to provide the right signals to each of the components of the business, so that collectively the organisation behaves in the most efficient manner.

But product economics and value chains and the competitive landscape all evolve relatively rapidly, and companies are left with structures that at best impede performance, and which all too often incentivise individual outcomes that are detrimental to the whole.

The simplest example of this is where one division within a company charges another division a commercial price which includes a profit margin. The logic of this is, of course, to ensure that each part of the organisation operates as a profit centre in its own right, driving for maximum efficiency and maximum competitiveness. This can, however result in the organisation as a whole pricing itself out of the market, by adding one too many layers of margin to its pricing schedule.

Beyond internal structures, whole business models can become outmoded, as technology or societal change or other developments undermine the basis on which products or services are sold or how customers are charged for them. Often the effects of this can take a decade or more to play out, and old world businesses can survive for a significant period without taking steps to adapt. This highlights the opportunity presented for new entrants to deploy new business models free from unwanted competition from the incumbents who could – if they chose or even realised – fight off the attackers if they were prepared to embrace a different world.

The music industry is one obvious illustration of this. Widespread access to broadband internet connections, and powerful mobile devices, mean that the notion of purchasing physical copies of recorded music has become entirely outmoded. Indeed even the outright purchase of individual songs, rather than simply renting access to a much larger library of music, seems anachronistic in 2013. Many new music services and models for access to music continue to emerge. Very, very few of these, however, are owned by the leading music retailers of the 1990s. Neither are there many owned by recording studios, who also had much more firepower to enter the online music segment than many of those who now have powerful businesses in this field. Thus technological change has led to a dramatic changing in licensing practices and who extracts the most economic rent from a particular activity.

The relatively slow pace of adaptation by one-time industry leaders also highlights the opportunity for one of these businesses to re-invent themselves, their products and services and cultures before they reach the corporate graveyard. In other words, even if it takes years for an organisation to adapt to a significantly changed environment, that organisation can still re-imagine itself and build a new, much more profitable future. Apple, under the renewed leadership of Steve Jobs between 1996 and 2011, is an obvious example, but there are others.

In practice, identifying deeply ingrained barriers to success in an organisation can be challenging, as it is often hard for companies that have been truly successful to recognise the need for change. And of course, implementing such a change can be costly and time-consuming. If a complete change of an organisation's culture is required, this will require particular skill. If such change is needed, then without it the organisation may simply die. So these challenges simply must not be ignored by Boards and management.

Happily there are warning bells which will ring loudly to warn you of the need for change. Major technological change is one, for obvious reasons. Sticking to tried and tested methodologies and strategies can be another. The emergence of a new type of small, fringe competitors that you're tempted to think of as irrelevant is a third. The last has become particularly critical in the world of the internet, where the absolute cost of launching a globally successful business can be very modest in some segments – many of the most successful and innovative companies of the last twenty years are under twenty years old.

Once you're prepared to look seriously for substantial barriers to growth, the key is to be able to step a long way back from the detail around what products and services a company provides and think about the core of the proposition to its customers. Once you are there, it is critical to listen to what your customers and your staff tell you – or indeed what they are not telling you. Of course you want the criticism much more than the praise, so you need to build the right relationships with customers and an internal culture that encourages new ideas and different thinking to flourish. If you do identify a need for a transformational or even significant change to your organisation, then it's important to be able to explore how this might be achieved at the most fundamental levels. This can, of course, be incredibly challenging.

A good example here is the world of print media, and in particular newspapers. The "Daily Universal Register" newspaper was firstly published in London in 1785, becoming The Times in 1788. It spawned many others with similar names, including the Times of India (1838), the New York Times (1851) and the Los Angeles Times (1881). These newspapers have continued in printed form to this day, with very little conceptual change to their formats over that time. In the UK, production processes changed dramatically in the 1980s, with the introduction of computerisation and direct to press print technologies, but the printed form remained the same.

In the late 1990s, however – after more than 200 years of an essentially status quo environment – the advent of the internet changed the landscape for print media completely. Most importantly, it became possible for a publisher to put news in the hands of its readers in real time, without any of the cost or complexity of overnight printing and national distribution networks. Since their formation, newspapers had raced to get the news to their readers before anyone else, as a key point of differentiation. Now they could deliver that news even more quickly, via web sites, making the competition for timeliness even more challenging.

Since then, a number of entirely predictable things have happened. Firstly, 3G networks were built and connected to smart phones (these technologies were already well established in the mid 1990s), meaning that people could receive news anywhere, anytime. Secondly, fixed line internet connection speeds increased dramatically through the introduction of ADSL and then ADSL 2 data transmission technologies. This meant that web sites could offer streaming video. Thirdly, ubiquitous data connections meant that any person could record and share news from anywhere with a mobile phone connection. Since social media platforms have emerged, it has become much harder – if not impossible – for news companies to report the news more rapidly than Twitter or Facebook.

This creates a series of fascinating challenges for newspapers. Should they stick with written content, or should they shift to much greater audio and/or video content. After all, the only reason that newspapers had only written content was that they couldn't do anything else. Should they continue to attempt to deliver news faster than anyone else? Or should they abandon the search for "news", and focus on comment and analysis? Should they stick with the traditional, two dimensional layout, where each item is chosen by the editor? Or would they be better to deliver content in a more flexible fashion that reflects the interests of each reader, delivering a home page that is entirely personalised? And how should they be paid? Can they continue with a cover charge – and its online equivalent of a pay wall – or should they seek digital revenue streams driven by consumer interactions with advertising content on their web sites. Thus neither news nor paper have disappeared as important from a consumer perspective, but the relevance of news delivered on paper had changed, meaning that the real value in print lies more in perspective and commentary than raw data itself.

The answers to these questions cannot realistically be found by looking at how the businesses operate today. They can only truly be explored by imagining a world ten years hence, where all online content globally can be filtered in real time to reflect an individual's particular interests, and delivered in a summarised form that provides a cogent editorial summary on each subject. The risk, of course, is that the technologies to do this will be well beyond the means of individual newspapers, meaning that people will turn to online specialists (Google, Yahoo and others that provide news services) for the curated, news-focussed content that traditional newspapers once provided. If so, the answer for global newsprint companies may be that they must merge with or sell to global internet platform operators, or run the risk of becoming steadily outmoded. The challenges are illustrated by The Times' own experimentation with pay walls. Following the introduction of charging in April 2009, visits to its web sites fell from 21 million unique users per month to just 2.7 million within the first year. Does this equate to a massive loss of value, or is the reduction in visitor numbers more than offset by the revenues being generated from the customers that remain?

Thus, if your business can describe very clearly its overall intended or likely strategic destination (more of this later), then it is frequently much easier for senior executives to identify some of the key milestones that would have to be achieved along the way. These milestones may be product or service related, or driven by positioning in particular segments, or represent a need for particular capabilities and experience. Or they may relate more deeply to cultural issues and the organisation's mindset. And, as in the example of traditional newspaper publishers, they may not necessarily be particularly attractive. Nevertheless, at least if you are realistic about the implications, you can make the best possible plans, adjust to the new environment and implement a new business model sooner rather than later. In other words you need to start with the future, and work back from there. Ignore the cash cows (which will more or less take care of themselves as long as they last), and implement hard and fast to position the business for the future, rather than to celebrate the past. Because the future is where the value lies.

CHOOSE THE RULES – BEWARE THE GAME

Once you've set your new business model in place, you should assume that your suppliers and employees and customers all play by the rules that you have written in to your business model.

Take for example the incentive structures of the global investment banks over the last 15 years. Even for mid ranking employees, half or more of remuneration was driven by short term incentives. For the most senior staff, as much as 99% was driven by bonuses. Bonuses were, of course, very sensibly linked to personal contribution and divisional profit and overall group returns. Meanwhile, a substantial proportion of revenues and profits were generated by proprietary trading activities, combined with equity and debt underwriting, both of which require the support of significant quantities of capital.

Risk and return are (or at least should be) linked, so the most profit will be made, over time, by taking the biggest risks. A logical game theory conclusion to this simple set of rules is that you would want to accumulate as much of someone else's capital as possible, and take the biggest risks reasonable, subject only to keeping hold of your job for long enough to collect the returns. Once you have been in the job long enough for the rewards of a single year's endeavours to be enough to retire on, your focus would become even more short term. If you were motivated purely by financial returns, it would be all too tempting to heap the entire bet on 27 red, collect the prize and return to the Bahamas. These were the rules of the game, written by the players themselves, and like every professional sport, funded by someone else.

Of course the real world is not quite as simple as this, and there are tens of thousands of people in the investment banking industry around the world who have worked long hours diligently seeking to deliver the best outcome for their clients and for their firm. It is simply ironic to note that the enormous financial losses incurred by these firms came about after they had taken in significant amounts of external capital, both in the form of external shareholders as well as investors in the funds managed by these organisations, and were no longer risking only the partners' capital.

LET'S MAKE OUR CLUB MORE EXCLUSIVE

Think also about the drive for corporate scale. On one dimension, larger companies with more diverse service offerings can provide more products to more customers at lower prices than smaller organisations. There are endless examples of how these cost curves work in real life – larger and larger call centres achieve lower and lower costs per call, albeit with slower and slower improvement as the centres become very large.

As a counterpoint to this, there are also plenty of examples where scale is a disadvantage, as lines of communication become too long, key employees become disengaged with their customers, and management becomes too far removed from day to day business. Companies suffering from this become unresponsive to customer needs, build up huge internal cost structures and in extreme examples become takeover targets for leaner, more nimble competitors. Alternatively, they become the ultimate victim of their own success, cross-fertilisation is replaced by inbreeding, and they simply fail.

From the perspective of a CEO who happens to be entirely focussed on personal remuneration, corporate consolidation means that there will be fewer and fewer top jobs, but they will most likely be better and better paid. Think about what happens in a bank takeover, for example. There have been literally hundreds of these a year in the US alone over the last 25 years. Typically the acquiror will pay a takeover premium of around 25% to 30%. In simple terms, this means that they will need to add 25% to 30% to the target company's profits in order to justify the price paid. Given typical banking cost structures, where around half of income is eaten up by costs, this will mean that costs will need to be cut by 20% to 25%. Incidentally, revenue synergies are usually left out of this equation, as they are notoriously hard to achieve and hence are kept entirely for the purchasers account, rather than being paid for through the takeover premium. Cost savings will typically be weighted a little more heavily towards systems and infrastructure costs, implying that staff costs (ie staff numbers) may only need to shrink by around 10% to 15%.

So what does all this mean for the employees? In practice, with a company that is achieving even modest growth, cutting headcount by 10% to 15% over a period of say three years may simply mean that there is no net increase in employee numbers over that period of time. Of course some jobs will change, and this will translate into both new jobs and redundancies, but the net effect may be zero.

But there will be 50% fewer CEOs!

Perhaps it is unsurprising, then, that CEO remuneration in the USA and a number of other countries has risen so strongly over the last twenty years, and certainly at much higher growth rates than average employee remuneration growth or growth in corporate profits. As a result, CEOs are now extracting a greater proportion of overall corporate profits than they did a decade ago.

In defence of CEOs, there are good arguments that large businesses have become steadily more challenging to manage, in part due to the accelerating pace of change in technology and consumer desires, not to mention the much more challenging environment than that seen in the 1990s.

Complexity and consolidation also suits the service providers – the larger and more complex an organisation becomes, the stronger the arguments the largest service providers will put forward that their customers need to hire the biggest and the best. The obvious risk here – for both the company and its service providers – is that they chase size over quality, attention and expertise. As a counterpoint to this, there are many examples of small companies with carefully tailored product offerings that have built global businesses operating in narrowly defined market niches.

So scale alone is not necessarily a great measure of success, and it is certainly not any guarantee of ongoing competitive advantage. The global PC market was dominated globally by Microsoft in the 1990s, with well over 90% market share in installed operating systems, a legacy of its founders' creativity, determination and commercial nous in developing and launching QDOS (as in "quick and dirty operating system", rapidly rebadged as "disk operating system" for obvious reasons) back in the 1970s. Today's smartphones are much more powerful than the desktop computers of only a few years ago, and as a result global market shares in computer operating systems are now shared between Microsoft (still strong in the declining PC and laptop markets), Apple and Google's Android. The latter two have a much stronger position than Microsoft in the rapidly growing mobile phone and tablet segment and so it is fascinating to watch whether Windows 8 and its close sibling Windows 8 mobile can secure Microsoft a stronger penetration into mobile devices.

ARE YOU LEGISLATING FOR GAIN OR PAIN?

Governments also get drawn into these games. There are countless examples of taxes and levies being introduced with well-intentioned objectives, only to incentivise for the wrong types of behaviour. A simple example is regulated pricing of services such as provision electricity or gas or water. Motivated by the very reasonable desire to protect consumers from price gouging by newly privatised utilities, the logical response is to regulate the cost to consumers. This inevitably means an investigation and appraisal of the reasonable cost of provision of those services, usually by an independent regulator. In assessing a reasonable level of permissible charges, the regulator will need to make allowance for operational expenditure, the need for capital expenditure to maintain and replace relevant parts of the infrastructure, as well as appropriate capital structures and the cost of debt. Typically these regimes result in determination of some form of agreed "regulatory asset base", with prices set so that, after costs, a reasonable return will be generated.

In the UK, the pricing windows were set in five year blocks, with an initial unit price being agreed and then indexed to inflation using an RPI – X formula. This meant that prices rose more slowly than the retail price index, meaning that they declined in real terms. The five year windows provided an incentive for efficiencies, with the companies benefiting during the pricing window from any super-profits generated. Prices were then reset after five years, returning further benefits to consumers. In a number of other countries, however, pricing resets have been determined annually. As the benefits of cost efficiency usually take up to a year to outweigh the associated implementation costs, in these markets there is no incentive at all for the operator in question to drive efficiencies. In other words, the structure of the market acts very effectively to impede efficiency.

In addition, in many countries it is hard to carry out a meaningful comparison of performance between closely analogous peers, either due to material regional differences in cost structures, or simply as a result of lack of information. Again, the UK approach was attractive, with privatisations creating 10 water and sewerage companies and 12 regional electricity companies. This allowed for very easy benchmarking of performance and efficiency.

Even so, regulators need to be on their guard. In one famous incident in the 1990s, the UK's electricity regulator OFFER concluded its pricing review and announced the new base price and price increase pathway for each of the 12 regional electricity companies. On the day of the announcement, the share prices all increased by around 50%. How could this possibly happen? It turned out that, quite through a quirk of near term share price movements driven by industry specific factors, and co-incidental but more or less matching movements by the UK stock market as a whole, the observed betas for the companies were all close to 1.0. Without getting into the technical details, this is much higher than would be usual for a low risk utility company. Consequently, encouraged by a well co-ordinated campaign by the companies concerned, the regulator allowed for a much higher cost of capital across the whole industry than was justified. This resulted in much higher price increases being proposed than would otherwise have been reasonable. Nevertheless, thanks to the fact that the companies were listed, this fundamental failing in the regulatory review process was exposed within hours. Thus the regulator was made aware of his error, and returned to carry out an additional, out of cycle pricing review the following year to correct his mistake.

INCUMBENTS 4, INNOVATORS 0

Ultimately many market structures have evolved over decades, adopting forms that may have been practical or opportunistic at a particular moment in time. They will of course have been shaped by the vested interests of the day, remembering of course that the person or business with the greatest profit ends up in the best position to shout with the loudest voice or exert the greatest influence by whatever channel.

Nowhere has this bias in favour of the incumbents been witnessed more clearly than in the tobacco industry, which has fought tooth and nail over many decades, supported by billions of dollars of annual profit, to preserve its business globally. Even today, now that the causal links between smoking and a series of cancers have been well established, the industry continues to battle to preserve its profitability for as long as possible.

Another interesting example comes from the field of alternative medicine. For a couple of decades, the world's largest pharmaceutical resisted the marketing of natural remedies such as vitamin C for colds, on the basis that there efficacy was not proven. Meanwhile the industry also argued that herbal remedies could never meet FDA requirements for testing, as they were based on natural, organic products whose precise chemical composition could never reliably be guaranteed. This compares to Western pharmaceutical products, which are manufactured by chemical processes which guarantee a precise composition. Eventually these organisations realised that there was more money to be made in selling such products themselves, rather than resisting their sale by others. Today, many sell a wide range of natural medicine products at prices equivalent to their conventional Western medicine equivalents.

The challenge comes about when it is a new market entrant – or new industry sector – that will be the winner, and incumbents will be the losers. In these circumstances, the siren voices of the past will be much louder and better funded than the innovators who have developed a better, cheaper, more sustainable and more profitable solution to a particular problem. The strength of forces such as this that are opposed to change can inhibit and indeed entirely undermine the ability of particular businesses or technologies to reach the economies of scale from which their old world competitors currently benefit. Thus to encourage true market efficiency, even the most free market of Governments need to invest resources in promoting both evolutionary and revolutionary change.

A very topical example of this relates to the energy sector, and in particular the use of coal and petroleum to power and light the world's homes, cars and factories. Many Western Governments have invested large sums of State funds in encouraging the evolution and development of conventional fuels and technologies.

Arguably the Chinese Government has done more than any other to support commercialisation of renewable energy technologies and drive them to full scale deployment. China already leads the world in both solar panel production and wind turbine production. Beyond substantial exports of these products around the world, China is investing heavily in deployment in its own market, all the while driving production costs further down the scale efficiency curve. For example, in response to the recent slowdown in installation of solar panels in overseas markets, China simply increased its intended installation of domestic solar in its home market.

Around the world, there have been voluble protests against this "intervention in the free market". It is interesting, then, to remember that the petrochemical industry itself benefits from huge Government support. For example, the OECD has compiled an inventory of over 500 measures that support fossil-fuel production or use in its 34 member countries. Between 2005 and 2011, these measures had a value of between US$55 billion and US$90 billion *a year*. These figures sound large, but they support an industry with combined revenues of some $4.6 trillion a year. Ironically this massive support for the status quo also represents a massive barrier to innovation, a vexing challenge indeed for many Governments around the world.

Finally, some of the worst failures of the free market have emerged in what in theory are highly regulated industries, at least in part because the fates of the poachers and the gamekeepers are too closely intertwined. The recent scandals in relation to the calculation of interest rates, such as LIBOR, represent just one example of this. Put another way, it is always worth spending a little time to think through all the vested interests, and who benefits most from a particular outcome.

As a child, I remember the introduction of breakfast cereals and orange juice as a "much healthier alternative" to the "old-fashioned" preferences for protein based meals based on eggs, bacon and a slice of wholemeal bread. Meanwhile, over the last twenty years, there has been a widespread shift towards low fat foods, not to mention many other products packaged and promoted as healthy. Examples include health bars (many of which have a fat content well over 30%, much higher than ice-cream), low fat yoghurt (frequently very high in sugar) and a range of other foods marketed as low in one thing when they are high in another.

These dietary shifts were fabulously profitable for the commercial organisations that manufactured and marketed these products. I suspect little real thought was given to the potential long run impacts on human health, as of course the effects of this in both a financial and personal sense were the direct responsibility of the organisations in question. Of course over the longer term these underlying societal factors do come to bear, and at least some of the major food manufacturers are now moving towards a deeper focus on health and nutrition.

How long would you wait for freedom?

The theoretical benefit of a free market economy is that these sorts of problems should eventually right themselves. The balance of power between tobacco companies, Governments and consumers has changed, and in the West smoking is no longer regarded as sexy, chic and sophisticated but rather carcinogenic and a burden on the health system. Indeed in Australia, regular smokers now make up just 16% of the male population, down from 72% in 1945. Smoking amongst women peaked at 33% in 1976 and is now as low as 14%. Smoking in nearly all public places is banned – not just indoors, but in a variety of public spaces, including many beaches too. But remember, this has taken decades to achieve. In the UK, 82% of men and over 40% of women smoked in 1945. By 2010, these figures had fallen to around 20%, very similar to the US (19%). Despite this, one of the top ten Fortune 500 companies is a tobacco company, showing just how a strong a grip on power the incumbents have.

Similarly, Western motor manufacturers are slowly moving to develop zero emission vehicles – led by long-standing visionary investment by companies such as Toyota, as well as mould-breaking new entrants like Tesla. Investment banks are beginning to explore whether it really is in their best long term interests to combine proprietary trading, capital markets activities and independent advice under one roof, or whether the collateral damage to corporate reputations brought about by the endemic conflicts of interest make it simply more attractive to separate each of these three businesses and set them free (Greg Smith's "Why I Left Goldman Sachs" tells one version of this story). Domestic appliance manufacturers now make enormously more power efficient products than 20 years ago and similar developments are under way in other industries.

The interesting point for many of these organisations is that very often it turns out that this more sustainable approach to business investment is more profitable and supports higher growth. The key is to understand where the structural barriers to better products or services or decision-making lie and work to change the structures themselves.

A neat example of this is national postal networks. In almost all countries, universal postal services operate on the basis of the sender paying to deposit the letter or package, with the recipient receiving the goods free of charge. The problem with this model is that the costs of operating the network are almost entirely fixed, whereas the revenues are completely variable as volumes change. This creates the perfect Catch 22 – reducing volumes of traditional mail mean that unit prices have to be increased, further reducing demand for postal services. At the same time, individuals continue to demand a universal, low cost postal service be provided by (or on behalf of) the Government. The solution to this is simple – switch to recipient pays model. Consumers would pay a flat rate to cover all inward mail received each year (at least within some "reasonable use" limits and constraints on junk mail). Consumers would benefit from lower marginal costs for receiving mail, and Governments would eliminate their exposure to rising fixed costs by indexing the annual charge for receiving post. Of course changes such as this are almost unthinkable in most industries.

In the meantime, a fundamental challenge for Governments and regulators and consumers remains. The free market only operates freely over the longer term – and indeed only then if barriers to innovation and competition are removed by legislation or policy action. So we must make sure we understand the implications of the rules of the game as we write them and rely on market forces to drive outcomes consistent with those rules.

As for the free market – rely on it to achieve optimal outcomes at your peril. In the fullness of time, the desired effects may indeed occur, but you may not live to see them.

5. The supremacy gene

CAN'T THEY SEE THE WRITING ON THE WALL?

Do you know a company that you are sure is doomed to fail? Preferably one that is currently riding high, but where you just know that, at some point in the near to medium term, it will go into terminal decline? I don't mean something as simple as a dramatically overvalued internet stock that will never generate the profits required to justify its current valuation. I mean a company whose products or services or business model is clearly outdated, and where its market share – or even its whole market – may well disappear in the course of a decade.

The impending energy revolution (of which more later) provides a rich seam of contemporaneous examples. Given the rapid ongoing developments in alternative energy, not to mention substantial investment by countries such as China, it appears increasingly likely that alternative power generation technologies will reach a point where they will be simply cheaper and more convenient than the fossil fuel alternatives. In more remote locations, including central Africa, tropical islands and mines in the Andes, solar power has reached the point where it is a cost effective alternative to conventional diesel-powered small scale generation. One major reason for this is simply because solar power doesn't rely on a long supply chain to deliver fuel, which is particularly costly if you are far from a refinery. And of course there are dramatic differences in the marginal cost of power production. Renewable sources such as solar and wind have very low operating costs once installed, which is already creating interesting dynamics in markets where these technologies contribute more than 10% of total power supply.

This trend towards much lower cost renewable energy sources will continue, and indeed within a decade (or at most two) solar power is likely to be cheaper than coal fired power, even without the imposition of a carbon price. This has implications for many companies and their business models. Beyond the obvious effects on the companies that mine and refine petroleum, think about filling stations. With the advent of electric cars, you have a convenient bowser at home, as you can simply plug your vehicle into a power socket in your garage. Even with current technology, an overnight charge of a Tesla Model S will be enough to power the car for a week's worth of driving by an average city driver. So you simply won't need local filling stations at all. Charging points will be needed in a few locations along long distance trunk routes, but the amount of energy (ie petrol and diesel) sold at retail shops will decline dramatically. Assuming there is no legislation to encourage a more rapid replacement of existing petrol-powered cars, the changes may take twenty years to work their way through the system, as cars have a long lifetime. But the eventual outcome – no more suburban filling stations – is clear now.

Of course there will be plenty of protests along the lines "But people like the convenience of filling their car at a service station!". Nothing could be further from the truth. People like the convenience of having their own car, but very few really enjoy driving to a service station to fill it up. Much more convenient simply to remember to plug in once a week or so at home.

People are, however, used to cars that have a range of 300 miles or more, and which can be refilled in a matter of minutes. They accept the inconvenience that you can't fill up at home, because that is all they know. If we were starting with a clean sheet of paper, the perception of this choice might be very different. One car would be much cheaper to refuel, could be conveniently refilled at home overnight with only seconds of your own time required, and would be much more environmentally friendly. The other would be more expensive to run, would mean that you had to buy your fuel from a store, and would pollute the environment. The only benefit the latter would offer is that you could refill quickly in the middle of a very long journey. Of course, rather than driving for six hours, stopping for five minutes and driving for another six hours, you might decide it was more sensible for the driver to have a rest, and stop for lunch for an hour, with your car happily recharging in the car park.

There are more subtle changes too – the combination of electric vehicles and low cost solar power mean that you can run cars far from a fossil fuel supply chain. And with far fewer moving parts to maintain and replace, even the servicing element may be simpler. This means a whole range of things become possible that haven't been before.

So it will be fascinating to watch how the various industry incumbents impacted by these changes behave. Some have embraced the opportunity – Toyota has been investing in electric vehicle technology for well over two decades, and several of the oil majors have been investing steadily in alternative power sources and renewable energy.

Others will simply fight hard to maintain the status quo. One example of the latter is the newfound enthusiasm that traditional motor manufacturers have for discussing range, rather than fuel efficiency, running costs or performance. Tesla's Model S looks rather good compared to its fossil fuel rivals on the last three measures. In contrast, range is likely to be of minimal relevance to a significant majority of drivers. Reflecting a typical suburban lifestyle, in many Western countries our cars travel an average of barely 250 miles a week. This means that we would only need to remember to plug them in once every ten days or so. Thus for most drivers, once range is over a couple of hundred miles (as it is with the Model S), it becomes an irrelevance. And even if you make a 600 mile trip in a day, would you really want to go without a stop for lunch?

This illustrates all too well how the structure of an industry, and the well-endowed business models of the past, can act to impede change. As a result, the free market's natural desire to move to a cheaper, better solution is slowed dramatically. As a thought experiment, think what might have happened if low cost, high capacity batteries had been invented by 1970, before the oil crisis. Would America have made the switch to electric transport then? And if it had, would the US be materially better off as a result of that change?

Fixed line telephone companies provide another good example. For a long time, they provided a critical line of communication - in a physical sense - for every house to the outside world. With ubiquitous internet services, including the rapid deployment of 4G mobile phone networks, the transmission of speech is almost a complete irrelevance for fixed line telephone providers in terms of the data capacity used. Happily for these companies plenty of people still rely on a physical phone line for its "reliability", although even this is unlikely to remain so for long. Meanwhile mobile phone services - a premium product only a decade or so ago - are now also viewed as declining businesses, with the emphasis moving rapidly to the services and content that can be provided over mobile broadband networks. So, whilst traditional telcos have done well in preserving their market positions in mobile phones and fixed line internet service provision, my guess is that they will become increasingly marginalised in the eyes of consumers, with all the value lying in the innovative devices they connect, and the entertainment and services that are provided.

Once again, this illustrates the impact of a changing market structure. Traditional telcos dominated due to national monopolies. But services and digital media can be provided very easily to a global audience, with very little starting capital. More innovative, faster moving competitors have seized this opportunity, creating businesses that in some cases are much larger than the domestic telephone monopolies. Telcos had the capital and security of cash flows to pursue these opportunities, but in nearly all cases would have found it highly challenging to imagine the nature of their new businesses.

More widely, how often do the major incumbents win? They have every opportunity to do so, as they have the money and market share to underpin their investment and thus reduce their own risk compared to a new entrant to the market. In truth, the answer appears to be rarely. So something is clearly wrong with how these companies make decisions and set strategy.

GREAT BUSINESS – SHAME ABOUT THE LEVERAGE

Foresight isn't just restricted to strategic or commercial matters – it can be about financing too. The last two decades have provided numerous examples of once great companies that have gone from corporate hero to the zero of bankruptcy protection in a matter of months. Non-banking examples include Worldcom (2002), General Motors (2009), Enron (2001), Conseco (2002), Chrysler

(2009), Pacific Gas & Electric (2001), Global Crossing (2002), Lyondell (2009) and Calpine (2005). In the Asian region, Australia saw the failure of its second largest airline (Ansett), a major insurance company (HIH) and a large telecommunications company (Onetel) all in the space of just a year.

In most of the more recent examples, the basic cause of failure was not a significant decline in operational performance, but rather reflected the effects of taking on too much debt at the wrong point of time. In other words, the core business was healthy and the financial structure was not. This is very much an internal failing – ie the failure was a direct result of decisions taken by the Board and management to accept significantly higher levels of borrowing, whether to "optimise the capital structure" or complete a "strategically significant acquisition" or otherwise to "return value to shareholders". In other words companies bowed to short term pressure to take decisions that would have a detrimental impact on the business over the longer term.

A more subtle version of this malaise was the use of surpluses embedded in corporate pension schemes to fund restructuring costs, for example by allowing early retirement at the fund's expense by older employees who were no longer required following a merger. This happened extensively in the early to mid 1990s in the UK, during a round of financial services and utilities consolidation. Whilst these surpluses were real at the time, many pension schemes have subsequently been left dramatically underfunded as a result of the sustained period of weak equity market performance that followed.

Corporate excess and corporate failure is nothing new, dating back to the formation of the earliest corporations. Early bankruptcies include the demise of the world's first company, the Dutch East India Company, which ended in bankruptcy in 1798.

Looking back to the previous major cycle of insolvencies in the 1980s, there was a much stronger bias towards broader corporate failure, driven by a weak economic environment, changing competitive dynamics and a lack of management action to reposition businesses and trim costs. This was particularly true in countries such as the UK and US, including once well-known names as Triumph Engineering (a British motor bike manufacturer), Atari Computer, Laker Airways (a low cost carrier that didn't have the firepower to outgun larger incumbents on the US/UK routes) and others.

It is interesting to speculate whether this shift from operational weakness as a cause of corporate failure towards financial weakness is a result of more effective operational management practices. The more likely cause, however, is the dramatically higher levels of leverage permitted and indeed encouraged by banks over the last fifteen years. These banks had, in turn, developed new ways to transfer this risk to third parties, making sure it was someone else that didn't have a seat when the financial music inevitably stopped and the credit crunch came. Either way, the potential for a substantial financial meltdown had been flagged well in advance, not least by a certain W Buffet and his commentary that derivatives were financial weapons of mass destruction.

BETTING AGAINST THE HOUSE – AND WINNING

Although they are supposed to be bastions of financial prudence and exemplars of good corporate citizenship, financial services companies have their own rich history of corporate disaster. Every decade has seen bankers find new ways to destroy ever larger amounts of capital in ever shorter time periods. In the 1970s, this took the form of excessive lending to Latin America, with a hangover that lasted for over a decade. Meanwhile the savings and loans crisis in the US in the 1980s saw the rescue of 747 financial institutions at a cost to the US taxpayer of nearly $90 billion. New home construction nearly halved, at least in part due to a significant reduction in the availability of credit. In the 1990s, the failure of banks such Nordbanken, BCCI and Barings rocked the European financial system and pointed to the need for significant reform. The last decade has seen a raft of failures and bailouts of some of the world's largest financial institutions.

I had my own window on one of these during my time at Barings in the 1990s. My time there started in 1994, in what was a golden age for the bank. It was top of the M&A league tables in the UK – then by far the largest M&A market in Europe – and was voted advisor of the year a number of times. By 1995, administrators had been appointed and the once extremely proud merchant bank had been acquired by ING for £1. The bank was brought down by a single trading position put on by a single trader, trading through the normal market and clearing house channels. The root cause was a simple, but abject, failure of governance and risk management, and indeed since that time there has been a dramatic overhaul of the regulatory supervision of the entire UK financial services sector.

The greatest bankruptcy to date, however, was the failure of Lehman Brothers, in the midst of the banking meltdown in 2008. The company filed for bankruptcy protection on 15th September that year, having failed to secure a buyer to rescue the group. Just a year earlier, the company's market value had peaked at over $60 billion. At its height, the company employed some 29,000 people in dozens of countries around the world. It was on the edge of joining the true global bulge bracket investment banking money machines, which then included Goldman Sachs, Morgan Stanley, Citi, Deutsche Bank, JP Morgan, UBS, Merrill Lynch and Credit Suisse.

Much has been written on the course and causes of the failure, but one point remains the most telling of all. How was it that Lehman got so close to the edge of failure that no-one could or would rescue the firm? Bear Sterns had been acquired by JP Morgan some six months previously, so there had been plenty of time for Lehman to orchestrate a solution. Merrill Lynch was shepherded into the arms of Bank of America, and even the then mighty Goldman Sachs and Morgan Stanley stood on the edge of the financial markets precipice for a few weeks. Meanwhile many smaller organisations were also saved during the global financial crisis, and this restructuring continues to this day, most recently with the emergency refinancing of Knight Capital, one of the largest market-makers in the US.

If Lehman was so powerful, why would no-one step in and buy the firm for a song? Was it the quality of the business, or its strategy, or its financial position, or simply the culture of its business and management? Keep these thoughts in mind as we explore further the perils of industry leadership.

THE BATTLE OF THE TITANS

A significant number of the world's largest and most successful companies simply didn't exist twenty years ago. This is true not just in the internet, but in technology more generally, as well as fields such as energy and financial services. Whilst some of the new leaders have been fashioned by an extensive series of acquisitions, others have grown almost entirely organically from garage start-ups. Many of the latter did so in the face of potential competition from one-time industry leaders that in practice never threatened them at all.

So how can it be that industry leaders – with all the internal resources that they maintain – can miss such substantial opportunities? Many industries around the world are led by iconic businesses that have battled for market supremacy for decades. Think of Airbus and Boeing, Coca Cola and Pepsi, Ford and General Motors, HP and IBM to name just a few.

As these corporate wars for customers and profit and recognition are played out, segment by segment, country by country, region by region, senior executives and corporate development teams work through their annual planning cycles looking for new ways to grow revenues, enhance operational efficiency and minimise the amount of capital employed.

Over the years, all sorts of strategic analysis and corporate planning tools and devices have been developed and are deployed in strategic reviews and corporate plans. This includes approaches such as:

-   SWOT analysis, considering the strengths, weaknesses, opportunities and threats facing an organisation;

-   Porter's "Five Forces", which adopts a slightly more rigorous approach, considering the threat of new competition, the threat of substitute products or services, the bargaining power of customers, the bargaining power of suppliers and the intensity of competitive rivalry;

-   Value chain analysis, which explores the nature and value-add of each activity that an organisation completes in providing products and services to its customers; and

–   Discounted cash flow valuations (enough said for now).

There are many other devices for developing overall corporate strategy, helping individual business units and divisions and whole companies to frame "strategy", including the various well worn methodologies of various consulting firms around the world. As with most scientific methods, these techniques are frequently used with little thought for the relative merits of the theories on which the techniques are based. This may seem harsh, but the truth is that these tools just provide a simple way for teams to express and explain the basic challenges that they are facing and to highlight areas of opportunity, very much as was intended by their creators.

Many of these tools are very much biased towards assessing what is happening in the external market in which the company is operating. They focus on customers and competitors, products and prospects, services and suppliers. Of course management teams are also conscious of the need to focus on organisational capabilities, reporting structures, bench strength, talent management and the like, and there are endless reviews of these too.

Beyond continuing to spawn a raft of new candidates for inclusion in games of buzzword bingo, these activities have also provided a rich living for external consultancies, as they seek new ways to "optimise performance". What they cannot readily do, however, is to examine the very DNA of the organisation itself, as created by the Chair, Board, CEO and senior management team. I single out in particular here the role of the Chair and CEO, as these individuals have a powerfully strong role in setting the tone and culture of the whole organisation.

So where can you look to find the warning signs of impending corporate weakness?

Corporate DNA testing

Making an impartial and searching assessment of the qualities of the Board and senior management of any large organisation is fraught with difficulty. Even with the UK's Cadbury Code, which places a nine year limit on Board terms, Board composition changes only slowly, and there is a real risk that Boards recruit only in their own image. Meanwhile, in cases of corporate excess or failure, it is much more common for the CEO to be fired or retired than it is for there to be a wholesale change of the Board as a first step towards renewal. And at lower levels in the business, most companies are much more likely to hire people that "fit" with the organisation, professionally and culturally, than they are to hire naysayers who think that the company is going about its business in the wrong way.

There are exceptions that prove this rule, the return of Steve Jobs to Apple being one obvious example, but they are relatively rare.

So what can you do if you start to suspect that your organisation does not quite live up to the internal rhetoric and external adulation of its biggest fans?

One place to start is by thinking about the overall corporate philosophy on which so many business processes and techniques are based. By this I mean the very frameworks by which we measure profitability, growth and success. Is your company a slavish devotee to the cult of financial rationalism? Are you and your colleagues confident that there are no serious concerns about the impact of changing industry dynamics, the effects of competition, or technologic innovations on your business? Do you sleep soundly knowing that your company has an enduring business model? Do your projections show that in ten years' time the company will be substantively the same as today? Do you think that ten year projections are pretty much irrelevant to corporate decision-making? Is everyone on your Board over the age of 50? Is the average tenure of your Board directors over five years? Do you think that it is the CEO's responsibility to ensure the bench strength of this or her team and their direct reports?

These are the questions that the insecure outperformer will be asking of themselves, more or less continuously, whether at a personal level or a corporate level. If you have answered yes to even one of the above questions, then alarm bells should start to ring.

And remember, corporate weaknesses at this level are like hypothermia. You may feel a little cold at first, but soon you stop noticing. At best you will end up with corporate frostbite, and at worst your organisation will die. So, if you believe that you've got all these bases well covered, you can be pretty confident that you and your colleagues are missing something of fundamental importance.

THE SUPREMACY GENE

The most severe threat to any organisation's future growth and profitability comes from within. The moment that a company starts to believe that its current strength and sophistication compared to its competitors is likely to be genuinely enduring, the rot sets in. People within the company become secure that they are the best executives in their industry and develop supreme confidence in their ability to manage effectively. They may also know that they, or their companies, have a strong track record of innovation, and are the industry leader that everyone else looks up to. If they think about it, they will probably conclude that they have the best overall business model too.

More than anything else, they know that they have got all the bases covered.

Meanwhile teams within the company know that their organisation delivers the best products and services. Indeed their company may have defined a whole industry, as well as the products within it, and all the other competitors are simply following in their (massive) footsteps. Employees will know that their company treats their people better than others, and that it is the most profitable in the industry. Quite likely they will expect the best salaries, and best bonuses, and best fringe benefits. Their friends and peers will admire them and their luck for working at such a great company.

This is the supremacy gene.

As with fish, the rot generally starts from the head, in the Boardroom, chief executive and senior management team. If it takes hold, this affliction breeds a particular form of corporate myopia so severe that the internal leadership team cannot perceive any future for the organisation other than perpetual industry leadership. In its most extreme forms, however, more or less any external commentator can see the seeds being sown for the imminent demise of the company in question.

Of course the death may be rapid, particularly if the culture has allowed outright fraud or similarly destructive behaviours to flourish. More often, however, the organisation will suffer a more lingering, creeping death. In a testament to the effectiveness of the free market, the share price will often come under pressure even before growth in top line revenues slows or margins start to come under pressure. Those who are close to the Board and management team will frequently hear a barrage of commentary from these individuals that "the market doesn't understand us". Of course the opposite is usually true – the Board and management may in fact have lost touch with the market sector in which they are operating, but financial markets have read the writing on the wall and are selling down the shares accordingly. Private companies do not have the same luxury of the stock market's early warning system, but the internal signs will be just the same.

Unsurprisingly, the supremacy gene breeds most effectively in monopoly situations, where the industry leader in question is exposed to little external pressure or competition. An obvious example is State run monopoly providers of utility services. Typically having a legislated cost plus pricing mechanism, there is no incentive for profit, and investment decisions are guided by factors such as security of supply and "national standards". It is not that these latter considerations aren't relevant – the point is that they only represent one aspect of addressing how best to deliver value for money to customers. The utilities companies of the UK of the 1980s provide great examples of this, employing vast numbers of staff delivering "critical" services "as efficiently as possible". With no external benchmarks, and significant economic and political power, these organisations were more or less a law unto themselves.

The subsequent privatisations were motivated by introducing external capital and hence allowing the rebuilding of Britain's then aging infrastructure without adding to the UK's national debt burden. These privatisations also created competition, either directly or through the ability to benchmark performance between more or less identical companies. Critically, they gave competition an incentive to work, through implementing regulatory pricing regimes that offered companies a share in the benefits of improved efficiency, as well as pricing windows that were long enough to allow these benefits to be realised.

SUCCESS BREEDS SUCCESS (AND MORE PAIN?)

But the supremacy gene can take hold elsewhere as well. Comfortable duopolies, and even some oligopolies, provide a fertile environment in which the gene will replicate.

Consider the case of my own home country, Australia. Over the last thirty years, it has achieved exceptionally strong economic growth, measured by Western standards. The population has grown by 49% to 23 million, and GDP per head has grown at around 4.5% a year to reach $43,000. It also benefits from an incredible amount of space. Despite populations in the major cities of four to six million, much of these conurbations are still made up of two story houses on the proverbial quarter acre block. And between the cities, population density is close to zero – it is nearly 700 km from Melbourne to Canberra and another 300 km to Sydney. Brisbane lies a a further 900km to the North. These four cities contain over half of Australia's population and their physical separation is substantial – Brisbane and Melbourne are 2,000 km apart, yet this is still the equivalent of just one twentieth of Australia's coastline.

So how can it be that Australia has become one of the most expensive countries in the world to live in? In part, of course, this is due to pressure on the housing stock, with average property prices having reached between $500,000 and $640,000 in the major cities. But more generally, the general cost of living is also incredibly high and visitors from cities such as London, New York and Tokyo remark on the high prices for almost everything.

It's not simply distance, or a small market, as many domestic commentators might have you believe. In practice, with much of the population living within 50 miles of three major sea ports (Brisbane, Sydney and Melbourne), anything other than highly perishable goods can be shipped by sea for modest cost.

Nor is it as simple as an over-utilised workforce, as employee sponsored migration programmes make it relatively easy to recruit workers from overseas where appropriate recruits cannot be sourced in the domestic market, although wage costs are admittedly high.

In a number of key industry sectors, Australia's economy, and indeed its competition regime, has bread a series of duopolies. These companies have flourished in a benign economic environment, achieving substantial turnover and profit growth, at least when compared to international peers. Examples include:

- Coles and Woolworths, Australia's two major supermarket groups, with a combined market share of something like 80%;

- These companies also happen to own Australia's two largest liquor retailers, not to mention two of the major fuel distributors;

- Suncorp and IAG, Australia's two largest personal lines insurers, with a combined market share of around 70%;

- Telstra, which still dominates in fixed line telephone service, and its major mobile competitor Optus (owned by Singtel);

- Westfield, which owns more major shopping centres than any other Australian property company

- Qantas and Virgin Australia, who together entirely dominate Australia's domestic air travel industry; and

–   ANZ, Commonwealth Bank, NAB and Westpac, Australia's "big four" banks, who have long been prevented from merging with each other to create their own duopoly under Australia's unofficial "Four Pillars" policy for banking. Between them, these banks control over 90% of all loans and mortgages.

The power of these market positions is demonstrated by the exceptional profitability of these companies. Although Australia is only the world's 52nd largest country by population, and 12th largest by GDP, it's leading companies are amongst the largest in the world when measured by market value. By way of example:

–   Both Coles and Woolworths are amongst the world's ten largest retailers;

–   IAG, QBE and Suncorp are three of the world's ten largest listed general insurers

–   ANZ, Commonwealth Bank, NAB and Westpac are amongst the world's top 25 banks;

On one level, this is a very proud achievement, and wonderful for Australians now in retirement living off the dividends generated by these companies.

But there is also a darker side to this success. These market values are, of course, the result of valuation multiples (which are unexceptional in world terms) and profits, which are particularly high. Importantly, the significant majority of the profits of these businesses are derived from Australia. So these profits also reflect costs to Australian consumers. This would be no bad thing if average selling prices to consumers were low, and the companies had achieved world-leading levels of efficiency. Sadly this is not the case – in many cases, like for like prices are materially higher. Hence, whilst on some measures these companies are moderately more efficient than their global peers, this is at least in part due to the higher prices being charged, rather than lower operational costs per unit.

Strong domestic market growth – driven by a powerful resources boom – and highly consolidated industries creates a significant risk of complacency amongst industry leaders. There is clear evidence of this in some areas. For example, well over a decade since internet shopping took off in earnest in the US, UK and other countries, Australia's largest department stores are only now beginning to launch full online shopping services.

But change does, eventually, follow. Virgin Australia has achieved significant growth in market share and profitability, through offering better quality and better service than its key rival Qantas, as well as innovations such as direct lounge access from the kerbside. This will, in turn, be good for Qantas too, as the two companies compete with each other to set new standards, driving better value for consumers, improved operational efficiency and sound returns on equity. And despite many complaints from Australia's retail sector about challenging domestic market conditions, a number of the world's largest fashion retailing groups, such as Zara and H&M are opening outlets in Australia.

You find these same issues around the world, repeated again and again. Think of the dramatic transformation of Kodak, once the world's leading photography business. I took my first pictures with a Kodak Instamatic camera – way up in the Himalayas on childhood family holiday that is still etched in my memory very clearly as a result of the pictures that I took. Today, barely even a shadow of the company remains, whereas its rival of yesteryear – Fuji – has remained a vibrant competitor.

CONSUMERS AND POLITICIANS ARE VULNERABLE TOO

In defence of companies, the supremacy gene affects ordinary people and politicians too. Again, the Australian example is telling, with Australian consumers lulled into believing that all was right with their world. They had the freshest food, world-leading service standards in their banks, impressive consumer electronics, department stores that were "never knowingly undersold", better choice than ever in the shops and they were able to afford premium cars from BMW and Mercedes. They liked visiting the local shops, and never much took to shopping online, other than for flights.

The last few years, however, have seen Australian consumers learn that they may not have had the full story. They discovered they could buy books and shirts and shoes and bicycles and consumer electronics offshore at a fraction of the price of their local department store, frequently with a much better range of choices, and delivery to their door.

In a moment of insanity, one of the big retailers complained very publicly about how consumers were avoiding the 10% sales tax on offshore purchases below $1,000. This simply highlighted to others how much money there was to be saved. Almost overnight, consumer confidence in retailers was shattered. No longer did a 50% sale look like good value – it simply highlighted that you'd been charged twice the reasonable price in the first place.

Of course the retail industry had built up a cost base to match the high prices charged for some goods – retail property rentals are amongst the highest in the world – and many companies have simply not learned how to optimise their use of online channels to improve efficiency. Ironically offshore retailers targeting the Australian market have been much quicker to adapt to the opportunities uncovered than domestic businesses with a strong brand and physical presence.

KILL OR CURE?

The supremacy gene was first identified as a concept by my colleague and wife Cassandra Kelly (a partnership that has been described as the ultimate M&A, but that will have to wait for another book). As she says:

"When you were a kid, your parents probably told you that no-one likes a know-all. There's a good reason for this.

When large organisations get to the point that they believe they are simply the best, they tend to close their doors to innovation, improvement and the ability to learn."

Just as the supremacy gene is brought about slowly through corporate inbreeding, the weakness can take a generation or more to treat. As with any psychological illness, the critical first step is, of course, simply to recognise that your organisation has been tainted and needs to change.

Starting from the top down, organisations needs to work to breed out complacency and any sense of permanence, and replace it with a more vigorous, dynamic and insecure culture. There needs to be wholesale change, not just in how you manage and set strategy for your business, but in how you think about what success in business really means. As we've already highlighted, there are some simple measures to be considered:

–   Work to longer timescales: Traditional financial rationalism has driven a particularly short term focus, which obscures the impacts of fundamental changes that are likely to occur in the medium term. Test your planning with the 2% challenge and start thinking now about how these anticipated changes can best be addressed;

- Embrace complexity: Be incredibly wary of strategies and business plans built on an assessment of base case projections – even if the business plans include some upside and downside sensitivities. Instead, seek to explore the whole distribution of possible outcomes, including the more outlying scenarios and look for tangible support to assess how likely they are to occur;

- Don't be afraid to combine these two: Very often the nature of revolutionary change is more predictable than its precise timing – if so, ensure that your business is positioned so that actual timing will not adversely impact you. Even better, find a way to be first and to harness the changes to your own advantage;

- Explore the impact of business models carefully: This includes your own business (and any in-built transfer pricing structures), as well as those of your competitors and the market as a whole. Look for ways to work with vested interests, rather than directly against them, just as pharmaceutical companies realised it was better to sell branded versions of homeopathic recipes than to fight their sale by others.

The good news is that, in many circumstances, changing market dynamics can be turned to your advantage. Often this will require a significant change in perspective. This may be as simple as thinking differently about how best to deliver products or services, or it may require the organisation to look at its opportunities from a different perspective. Over the longer term, the upside opportunities will almost always outweigh the near term challenges and costs of transformational change.

6. The energy revolution

TIME TO LOOK IN THE MIRROR

So far we have explored how the world's religious conversion to financial rationalism has driven an obsessive focus on the near term that has held organisations back from pursuing otherwise incredibly profitable growth pathways. We've also drawn attention to the inability of business school 101 project and company evaluation methodologies to grapple properly with the complexities of the real world, making it it hard if not impossible to make proper allowance for the benefits of innovation.

Looking at more structural factors, it is clear that the free market does not necessarily drive the best solutions over the near term, even from a purely commercial perspective. Indeed individual companies and whole markets can be prevented from achieving profitable growth by their own structures, often created as an accident of history (or previous vested interest).

Finally, I've urged you to test your organisations for presence of the supremacy gene. Generated by corporate inbreeding, it leads to the insidious complacency and self-satisfaction that can destroy the largest companies over the space of a few years.

Put all of these factors together, and you have the perfect recipe for a set of pre-conceptions about the future that will inhibit innovation, stifle renovation and neuter creativity no matter who runs the business or who you recruit to your team.

With this in mind, what better place to put these theories to the test than in re-exploring the highly controversial debate about carbon pricing, climate change and the benefits of changing the world's energy habits to break the reliance on fossil fuels, and switch entirely to zero emission, renewable and environmentally responsible energy sources.

To judge by the world's media and much of the conversation around boardroom tables, the vast majority of people in business believe that this change will be incredibly expensive to implement, will increase ongoing energy costs, and thus create an additional and painful economic burden that most countries are currently ill-placed to sustain.

If you feel this way, ask yourself how much of this presumption is grounded in objective analysis of appropriate facts and research, and how much reflects your experience or pure gut feel? Then ask yourself whether these are really the right measures.

GOOD THINGS NEVER LAST FOREVER

Oil and gas have been fundamental to global economic development for the last hundred years or more. At current rates of consumption of around 90 million barrels a day, or 33 billion barrels a year, there are sufficient reserves to last at least several decades, and potentially longer. This sounds like a long time. But if you've read chapter two, you'll now be starting to wonder what your grandchildren are going to do for light in the evenings or plastic bags, unless of course you've dusted off your Brealey & Myers corporate finance textbook and discounted future generations to zero.

Seven of the top ten companies by revenue included on the 2013 global Forbes 500 list are energy companies. These are all oil and gas companies and operate globally. Their products quite literally power most of the world. The combined annual revenue of the top twenty oil and gas companies globally is over $4.0 trillion US dollars, more than the GDP of all but the world's three largest economies. In other words, energy from fossil fuels represents one of the largest single costs in the world economy.

Together, the top 20 companies have a market capitalisation of some $2 trillion. Now, market value isn't the only measure of importance. But to stock market investors and most of their investment management advisors, it provides the basic starting point for how your portfolio should be weighted. Most funds compare current fund weightings with a "neutral" weighting, not least because of the widespread paranoia about the need to ensure performance does not fall below the relevant benchmark. Of course the neutrally weighted portfolio may deliver truly lousy performance, but that's not as bad (from an investment manager's perspective) as underperforming the index.

So, in market value terms at least, energy is one of the most important industries in the world. It's certainly significantly more valuable than the world's agricultural sector (much of which isn't listed). It's also much more important that agricultural science or drug development or technological innovation, much of which is barely captured in the value of listed companies.

But the power industry is critically dependent on a natural resource which has a very short shelf life compared to the history of the world. And of course substances such as oil and gas have been used for other purposes, such as the manufacture of plastics and fertilisers, so devoting them largely to use as fuels seems illogical. And even if solutions such as carbon capture and storage could reduce the environmental burden of fossil fuels, we know with absolute certainty that these fuel sources will eventually run out.

With this in mind, it seems incredibly logical to make real efforts to reduce dependence on fossil fuels sooner rather than later. Indeed, as has been well publicised in recent years, at the least it would be sensible to move towards a more level playing field and eliminate the substantial Government subsidies that still exist that provide financial incentives to promote the use in favour of fossil fuel technologies over more modern, cleaner and renewable alternatives.

Now, if you're not a believer in climate change, or you think that the underlying issues will be resolved by technological evolution in due course, please do persist with this chapter. Its real purpose is not to argue these issues themselves but to demonstrate the potential for a significant paradigm shift.

If you do think that these issues have potential to drive significant near term shifts in thinking, then it would also be incredibly logical to start examining some of the associated financial risks. For example, many of the world's larger savings and insurance-related investment pools have significant investments in fossil fuel assets – much larger than their investments in alternative energy sources. A number of academics, actuaries and other professional services organisations are beginning to examine these risks and it will be interesting to see how rapidly this translates into investment decisions. Certainly in 2012 and early 2013 there was a substantial reduction in the valuation of many fossil-fuel based resources companies, but it remains to be seen whether this is temporary or permanent in nature.

IF YOU WANT TO PLAN FOR THE LONG TERM, WHY NOT START NOW?

As a power source, fossil fuels are also damaging to the environment – indeed, if the world's politicians wanted to restrict global warming to just two degrees, then we would need to stop using fossil fuels entirely within about ten years. Despite these risks, a significant proportion of the world's savings are invested in these companies. In the language of financial services risk management, the entire world economy, and indeed the entire world savings and investments pool, is exposed to a substantial basis risk.

This risk is energy, or rather the source and cost of energy. And irrespective of your views on climate change, it remains critical to factor in the potential for dramatic changes in the cost of energy. The pessimist's view is that energy will become much more expensive if we are "forced" to change to renewable energy, and that this will create an enormous economic burden. So at one extreme, you might factor these scenarios into your analysis. The optimist, on the other hand, will see the opportunity - or even probability - for much *lower* cost power. As one example, the cost of solar power has already fallen dramatically over the last few years, and this technology is still relatively early in the development cycle compared to coal and gas fired power stations. So at the other extreme, you should also factor in scenarios in which the cost of energy falls significantly from current levels. These scenarios should also allow for the fact that this energy will have a very low marginal cost once the generating stations are built, as their fuel (wind, rain or sunshine) is free.

My own view, for what it's worth, is that further step reductions in the cost of renewable energy appear certain over the next three to five years. And over the medium to long term, this energy revolution will lead to material upside for economies as a whole.

This need to explore widely divergent scenarios for the cost of power was brought into sharp resolution in 2009 as we were working through the valuation of Geodynamics, the world's leading "hot rocks" geothermal energy company. Pottinger built a highly sophisticated valuation model, utilising Monte Carlo simulations to explore a wide range of scenarios as the company's development programme unfolded and the world economic environment continued to change. This approach allowed us to explore many of the uncertainties that would impact value over the medium to long term in a statistically robust manner.

As our work progressed, we uncovered that virtually all analysis that had been carried out to evaluate such companies and projects used a single, central set of estimates for electricity prices over the medium to long term. Most importantly, these estimates assumed that power prices would increase only very marginally in real terms over the next fifty years. This seemed inherently unreasonable, not least because UK domestic gas prices had just been increased by nearly 60% literally overnight. For the record, if prices increase at a compound rate of 1% a year, it will take 48 years for them to increase by 60%. In other words, a 60% rise overnight is more or less the same increase as was being factored in over the course of half a century in all the standard models. Unsurprisingly, if you factor in modestly higher rates of price increase – driven for example by an increasing carbon price – then you will rapidly reach very different findings in your financial models.

Of course we highlighted this risk – and both the upside and downside outcomes of material changes in the course of world energy prices. And unsurprisingly the valuation range for the company in question was very wide.

Happily, from a technical perspective the company's exploration and development programme has progressed well and its first demonstration geothermal power plant is operating successfully.

From a commercial perspective, however, substantial reductions in the cost of other sources of energy have placed downward pressure on prices. Taken together, these factors mean that the organisation has achieved technological success, but is unable at this stage to deliver large amounts of renewable energy to the Australian national grid at a price which would be competitive with other forms of power. There are, however, potentially attractive applications for remote power, and the technology remains tantalisingly close to offering a cost-effective source of zero-emission base-load power from a renewable resource.

Whatever your views on renewable energy, there are some very significant vested interests at stake. Short term, the companies want to maximise their profits and the value of their resources. Investment bankers want the companies to do more deals (and love volatility). Construction companies want to build new mines and railway lines and ports. Banks want to finance these projects (as long as they are sure they will be repaid). Financial advisers and investment managers want share prices to move up. Consumers want the cheapest power. Politicians want to get re-elected.

Longer term, the picture is rather more complex. Eventually fossil fuels will run out and will have to be replaced. The more fossil fuels are burned in the meantime, the greater the downstream environmental challenges and business and consumer costs will be incurred. Meanwhile renewable energy is rapidly becoming competitive with traditional fossil-fuel sources, and indeed is already materially cheaper for uses such as remote power.

The point here is not about the rights and wrongs of whether and how to respond to climate change. Rather it is to focus on your perceptions of when and how these issues might eventually be resolved, whether through the forces of economics or environmentalism. Whichever it is, the impact on power prices and future power price inflation is likely to be profound, and you need to factor this in.

BEYOND FINANCIAL ARMAGEDDON: THE WORLD OF ILLUSORY GROWTH

Many Western economies have been almost frozen by the after-effects of a decade of illusory growth that was fuelled by ultra-cheap finance. Throughout this period, funding costs were at very low levels, and investment appraisals were based on the lowest discount rates seen for half century or more. It is ironic, then, that so much weight was placed on near term returns, as low interest rates increase the importance of longer term outcomes in financial models.

A number of years have passed since the beginnings of the global financial crisis, and many governments and boards around the world are struggling to find ways to deliver a "return to growth". Given the severity of these challenges, it is perhaps unsurprising that issues related to sustainability can be perceived as a necessary but externally imposed cost. Measures related to climate change in particular are all too easily seen as an economic ball and chain, slowing growth and bringing unnecessary cost at the most challenging point in the economic cycle. With this in mind, could the polarised and at times vitriolic corporate and political debate in countries like Australia be blinding corporations and Governments to a significant opportunity for profitable growth, which would drive business and economic outperformance over both shorter and longer time scales?

In part, the negative attitudes towards some of these issues in boardrooms reflect the genesis of many of the environmental campaigns. Action groups focussed on environmental activism, diversity, climate change, organic farming and other causes have their roots in 50 to 100 years of protest movements, typically led by campaigners from the fringes of corporate society. So, whilst many of these issues have quite rightly moved into the mainstream of business and Government, there is a long standing historic context of conflict, confrontation and mistrust.

STOP THINKING OF ELEPHANTS

Advocates of change must leave this history behind, however socially important it has been, and frame the opportunity in a way that focuses on profitable growth and improved efficiency. Lakhoff's book "Don't Think of an Elephant" highlights how much of the socio-political debate in the US is framed within a frame of reference that is particularly favourable to one set of political values. In the same way, you must be on your guard against presuming that resolving a particular set of issues can only lead to a negative outcome.

Without any doubt, the next ten to twenty years will see dramatic changes in the way that mankind generates and uses energy. This will be as transformational as the IT revolution of the 1970s and 1980s and the mobile communications revolution which followed. Don't start by thinking about how difficult this sounds. Instead focus on what would become possible if power could be generated more cheaply than at present, without producing greenhouse gas emissions or having any other environmentally damaging effects. Of course, our environment would become cleaner, especially those cities around the world that currently suffer from very high pollution caused by fossil fuels. Energy intensive products, including travel and transport and simply heating your house, would become cheaper. If power was cheap enough, water could economically be desalinated for use in areas currently suffering from severe water shortages. Dependent on the approach adopted, the solutions found may create further virtuous circles, creating knock-on benefits. As an example, electric cars could be connected to the network when not in use and provide a ready solution for mass storage of energy from intermittent sources of energy such as solar power.

Technology, know-how and practical experience already exists that would allow radical change in terms of energy costs and operational efficiency across a number of key industry sectors, including power generation, food production and shipping. In many cases the cost reductions will be immediate and the payback periods are short. There are also other tangible benefits that would flow, in terms of environmental impact, social perceptions and employee engagement.

Of course in exploring these opportunities, you must be on your guard against judging the potential of new technologies using measures that are relevant to the past. A great example here is motor cars and the potential for a switch to all electric vehicles. It is fascinating to observe that, if you raise the subject of electric cars in a general conversation, people will typically question whether they have the range to be a realistic replacement for a conventional car. This seems intuitively logical – although if you think back you'll remember that it is only quite recently that motor companies have started to focus on range rather than fuel efficiency.

But stop for a moment and ask this – how far does the average driver drive in a week? If you don't know the answer to this question, then you simply don't have the information to know whether range is really a material issue at all when deciding to choose an electric car over a petrol car. The US Department of Transportation helpfully provides data on this, which shows that the average person drives about 13,500 miles (about 21,600 kilometres) a year. This only about 260 miles a week! In other words, if you're the proud owner of the new Tesla Model S all electric car, you'll need to remember to refuel just once a week. Of course, unlike a petrol car, you can do this at home, simply plugging the car in. Oh, and it's way cheaper to refuel than with gasoline as well.

Of course the response to this is "What about those long distance journeys?". Again, US Department of Transportation data shows that virtually all journeys are under 100 miles long – less than 0.5% in fact. This means that very few journeys will ever require you to find a place to charge whilst you are en route. Even better, Tesla is setting up recharging stations on long distance routes. These are powered by solar power, meaning that there is zero marginal cost when you fill up. Tesla passes this on – so the charging stations are free to use. A traditional car manufacturer could never offer this benefit, as there is a real cost to supplying each extra gallon of fuel.

The point of all this is to bring to life a simple observation. When people talk about range of cars, many people will get drawn into agreeing that range is of course an issue (which it is), without ever considering the relevant facts about how range would impact them in reality. As an example, the 11 hour, 540 mile drive from Sydney to Melbourne would probably require a single one hour stop for lunch (very sensible to avoid driver fatigue in any case) and – maybe – a quick coffee later in the day. So the factor you think about – or are encouraged to think of by the vested interests that favour the status quo – may actually turn out to be a benefit of the new technology when seen through a slightly different lens.

The wide-spread adoption of renewable energy sources will not be without its challenges. The design of existing electricity networks and markets is based on a paradigm which combines a mix of base-load power (which is always available) with more flexible peak load power to ensure that demand for power can be met through-out the day. Together, conventional base-load and peak load power generation capacity can deliver power as and when it is needed. The same is not necessarily true for renewable energy – for example solar and wind power are both dependent on environmental conditions. On the other hand conventional power sources have marginal costs of production – that is to say that the more power they generate, the higher the associated costs (they burn fuel). Renewable sources have minimal marginal cost – essentially nothing more than wear and tear on the turbines, meaning that their marginal cost of production is very close to zero. And finally, small scale, local power production (such as roof-top solar panels) is becoming increasingly viable, meaning that power is being generated much closer to where it is used.

Together, these factors will create an entirely new set of challenges in ensuring that power is available when and where it is needed. There are significant implications for the design and management of local power grids and national transmission networks. In addition, there may well be dramatic impacts on the dynamics of power pricing in electricity supply markets, as in some weather conditions large amounts of power will be available at very low marginal cost to the generator.

In short, a transition to renewable energy is almost certain to create new paradigms, and may also lead to lower cost energy and other benefits. It may not be about increased cost at all.

IS THERE THAT MUCH TO LOSE?

The great revolutions in technology (in the broadest sense of the word) have typically brought a significant leap in economic prosperity over periods of just a decade or two. Basic standards of living in terms of food, water, sanitation and healthcare have increased significantly for many people. And, particularly over the last century, there have been significant benefits for quality of life and lifestyle in both the developed and emerging markets.

Whole new industries have emerged, and existing businesses have been dramatically restructured or disappeared. Machinery replaced manual labour in the industrial revolution. Cars and tractors replaced horses. Aeroplanes replaced passenger liners. Computers replaced typewriters. CDs replaced records. The iPod and iPad created a trillion dollar market for a new kind of mobile device. Downloads replaced CDs. Now ubiquitous broadband is allowing cloud services to replace downloads. Mobile phones are replacing cameras.

An important lesson of this history is, of course, that those who do not adapt early to the new paradigm may well not survive. For example, widespread 3G data services spawned the smartphone, the first mobile device that was more a computer than a telephone. Over the last decade, Apple's market value has increased from $10 billion to over $600 billion. In contrast Nokia, then the global leader in phone handsets, saw its market value decline to a low of just $3 billion.

In purely market value terms, the world's largest energy companies have something like $4.6 trillion at stake. To date, their actions show clearly that they recognise the risks involved. Unsurprisingly, the last five years have seen a massive increase in attempts by these companies to monetise their assets. More coal and petroleum and gas projects are under development now that at any time in the history of man. Of course in part this is driven by growing demand from India and China. But that is only part of the story. If you believed you owned a scarce resource that had a long life you would logically take a very measured approach to development, as OPEC has done over the last fifty years. In contrast, significant new resource projects are being brought on stream at a breakneck pace. In Australia alone, investment in new resources infrastructure peaked at around $100 billion *in a single year,* and reached over 8% of GDP (roughly four times the long run average). And owners have also been selling assets where they can, to those that absolutely have to have security of supply over the near to medium term.

Commodity prices also tell a similar story, with petroleum and coal and gas prices trading well below their record highs of a few years ago. Indeed peak oil and peak coal prices may already be behind us, with gas cking out a slightly longer future as it offers emissions only half those of coal.

And academics, financial investors and environmental campaigners are all examining the potential effects of the anticipated migration away from fossil fuels. As just one example, the Institute of Actuaries in the UK is working with academics from Anglia Ruskin University to explore how the world's system limits (as originally laid out in the book "Limits to Growth" in the 1970s) might impact on the global financial system.

Will Your Company Miss The World's Next Great Revolution?

In our crystal ball, we see very substantial economic benefits accruing to those who can ride the energy revolution successfully.

There have already been dramatic advances in the power efficiency of many devices, as well as the storage of electric power, driven by the needs of mobile devices and laptop devices. These can be leveraged in other industries, and indeed the world's first mass production all electric car has batteries that are based directly on laptop technology.

Global organisations such as GE have already adopted this mindset, focusing on the opportunities that the energy revolution presents, to move to a new growth paradigm. Meanwhile other major companies are adopting strategies to better position themselves for this energy revolution. As a simple example, Rio Tinto, one of the world's largest resources companies, announced the sale of around 30% of its global aluminium refining business, proposing to exit nearly all its conventionally powered smelters, and retaining those run by hydro-electricity.

None of this is science fiction. Nor does commercial implementation necessarily require any material further technological or scientific invention. But there are some critical barriers to be overcome, which illustrate perfectly the issues that we've been exploring.

Firstly, there are numerous examples where industry structures create a mis-match between who makes the investment and who reaps the reward. In my previous example of domestic refrigerators, for example, it took a global energy efficiency labelling scheme to unlock investment by manufacturers in technology to deliver lower energy fridges, allowing consumers who purchased these items to reduce their power costs. A similar approach has been adopted in relation to water use in domestic washing machines, and indeed consumers have long understood the benefits of purchasing a fuel efficient car. In many cases, there is upside for all stakeholders in addressing these challenges, implying an important role for industry bodies and Governments to play in educating consumers and providing objective and reliable information to allow them to make informed decisions.

Changes in technology can lead to significant paradigm shifts which address these industry structure challenges. As discussed earlier, Tesla Motors' customers who do make those rare journeys of over 300 miles, can refill for free at a Tesla recharge station. These few remaining filling stations become an additional touch point – and an additional service – for Tesla's customers. No conventional fuel-powered car manufacturer could ever afford to offer free petrol to every customer on these journeys.

This is where the 2% challenge to your strategic thinking is so helpful, as it will highlight parts of your business where inflexion points are approaching. In the case of Tesla, that turning point may already be here, with investors driving its share price significantly higher, a striking recognition that the company has created a vehicle that is simply better on many measures than its fossil-fuel powered competitors.

The second challenge is the continuous focus on short term timescales, which of course also impedes free market forces from navigating the barriers created by industry structures. Virtually all major business decisions reflect at least in part consideration of some type of discounted cash flow methodology. With an equity discount rate set at 10% and a long term growth rate of just 3%, pure mathematics typically places half the weight or more on the first ten years. As a result, investments that provide a pathway to a strong market position over the medium to longer term are often ignored in favour of short term profitability. At 15%, the weighting increases to two thirds. Hold those figures in your mind for a moment.

If you focussed on just the next five to ten years, you'd never start down the pathway of innovation. The benefits would be too remote and the costs too uncertain. As the years went by, you would get closer to the point in time where starting to invest would surely make sense. By the time you reached it, nimbler and more far-sighted competitors would already be five to ten years ahead of you in developing the technology. We've seen this play out in real life with companies like Nokia and Kodak, and the same may well happen again with motor manufacturers.

The third challenge is complexity. It is genuinely hard to predict the likely pathway for battery technology evolution, or for petrol prices, or other factors that influence consumer choices regarding which vehicle to purchase. In addition, there is the ever present risk of Government intervention, offset by the very slow changes that occur in the national "car park ", as typically cars have a life of ten years or more. The only solution to this is to embrace the complexity in operating environment that it implies. Build teams of people who are not afraid to question the status quo, and who have the confidence to challenge anyone in the organisation (respectfully of course). And build statistical analysis of risk and uncertainty – including in relation to technological innovation – into your planning processes and financial modelling.

Finally, make sure that everyone in your organisation knows that you don't have all the answers. Watch out for the signs of the supremacy gene in every strategic planning meeting that you attend. And if you have visionary team members who want to spend time thinking about things that seem unpredictable today, you must encourage them to do this. Then listen carefully to what they say.

Focus on how such radical innovations could be made real, rather than on the barriers to success.

So why did I pick a subject that has generated as much controversy as climate change to illustrate the power of these tools? I think there is no better illustration of a highly complex challenge. If you apply the 2% challenge to problems where the source and cost of energy is a material consideration, you will almost certainly identify that there will be an inflexion point by when your organisation will need to switch from an unthinking reliance on the perpetual availability of "low cost" energy from fossil fuel sources to exploring alternatives. In exploring when and how to do this, base case modelling is unlikely to help, as there are many variables and uncertainties arising from rapid technological change. The constraints of existing industry structures have dramatically restricted our evolution in some areas, and the incumbents are able to mount noisy, well-funded campaigns designed to delay the inflexion point as long as possible. This creates value for them, but may be destroying value for the world's economy as a whole.

And if you're reading this and thinking "I don't think this really applies to my organisation...", then are you sure that you too aren't suffering from the early effects of the supremacy gene?

Together, these factors illustrate more broadly that conventional decision-making – based on a slavish belief in the power of financial rationalism – is fundamentally flawed. In short it is too one-dimensional, and simply is ill-suited to a world that is changing so rapidly. So we should reflect on its life, remember the good parts, and then bury it for good.

7. An obituary for financial rationalism

THE ORIGIN OF CAPITALISM

Since the formation of the world's first stock companies in the early seventeenth century, businesses have sought to grow profits, build empires and make their owners rich.

Over the centuries, corporations have wielded enormous economic power and political influence, and they have built management and operational infrastructure to rival that of some of the world's largest nations. Walmart, currently the world's largest company by headcount, employs more than two million people directly, and many more indirectly through its supply chain – dozens of countries have smaller populations than this. Exxon Mobil, the world's largest company by turnover, would rank as the world's 27th largest country in terms of GDP. The cash holdings of Apple computer have from time to time been larger than those of the US Government. And the notional principal associated with the debts of Lehman when it failed was greater than all but the largest of the world's economies.

An enormous amount has been achieved by corporations. They have built motor cars, put computers on nearly every desk, mobile phones in nearly every hand, and brought high quality healthcare to a significant part of the world's population. Long distance travel now takes hours, not months, and is cheaper than ever before. Cars, in the form of the Tata Nano, can now be purchased in India for around $2,000. And before long, most people in the world will have access to more or less the sum total of human knowledge through a search engine on their mobile phone – a modern day Library of Alexandria, free and open to all, in your pocket.

Over the centuries, growth has come in many forms, with each new corporate paradigm apparently more clearly focussed than the last. And as each age has come to an end, the failings of the previous paradigm have been clear for all to see.

THE BIRTH OF THE CORPORATION

The world's first true joint stock companies were the British East India Company (granted a Royal Charter by Queen Elizabeth in 1600) and the Dutch East India Company (founded in 1602). These companies were both formed to exploit the prospective riches to be generated from newly discovered countries in the Far East, increasing their power by acting as domestic monopolies for the so-called "Spice Trade". These opportunities were opened up by revolutions in shipbuilding over the previous century or so, which had enabled the construction of larger ships better able to tackle circumnavigations through almost entirely unchartered waters and to return with cargo.

The India Companies' early trade was in goods such as cotton, silk, tea, opium and spices. These companies secured very strong positions in trade with these regions, and indeed the Dutch East India Company held an absolute monopoly on all trade with Japan for over two hundred years from 1640 to 1854.

The Charter of the British company – originally the "Governor and Company of Merchants of London trading into the East Indies"- gave it a fifteen year monopoly on trade with all countries east of the Cape of Good Hope and west of the Straits of Magellan. This legislated monopoly was subsequently extended indefinitely (so long as the company remained profitable) and continued in various forms (and following a merger with a second East India Company) until the late eighteenth century. In practice, the company pursued trade with the Indian sub-continent, including what is now India as well as parts of Pakistan, Iran and Afghanistan and at various times in its history effectively assumed economic and political control of most of India as well as other territories. It struggled, however, with the oversight of what was, in effect, a substantial political and economic empire and was nationalised following the Indian Mutiny in 1857. The company was eventually dissolved in 1874.

The Dutch East India Company's fortunes were centred on the region now know as Indonesia. It established a base by the name of Batavia (modern day Jakarta). Eventually the Dutch East India Company became bankrupt as a result of corruption and was wound up in 1800. Its assets and debt were taken over by the government of the Dutch Batavian Republic and its various territories became the Dutch East Indies. These were expanded during the 19th Century to include the whole Indonesian archipelago, eventually becoming the Republic of Indonesia.

Other organisations from this early period remain in existence and independent ownership to this day. The UK's insurance market, Lloyd's, began its life in 1688 at Edward Lloyd's Coffee House. Starting out as a place to buy marine insurance, it has evolved into the world's leading specialist insurance market. Just a few other examples include Grolsch (1616), Fiskars (the Finnish knife and scissor company 1649), Bank of Scotland (1695) and Sotheby's (1744).

GLOBALISATION AND THE DAWN OF EMPIRES

The nineteenth century saw a dramatic upturn in corporate fortunes, with the industrial revolution driving dramatic increases in economic productivity, leading to exceptional wealth and power for the entrepreneurs that seized the opportunities presented. There are hundreds of well-known companies that remain successful to this day that can trace their formation back to the nineteen century. They span many countries and industries and include names such as Bausch + Lomb (1853), Cargill (1865), Citibank, HSBC, Levi Strauss (1873) and Bechtel (1898). These companies remain powerful to this day, and have every opportunity to thrive for another hundred years so long as they can continue to adapt to the changing economic and political climate around the world.

The turn of the twentieth century saw the beginnings of a dramatic increase in the rate of innovation. Although the world still moved to a much slower beat than today, the first thirty years of the twentieth century saw both the end of the old British Empire and the beginnings of an entirely new world order in economic, political and technological terms.

Looking back on this era, the business culture of the day was much more focussed on stability and growing profits, no doubt influenced by the fact that many more of the largest companies remained privately-owned compared to the modern world. Time value of money – and the obsessive focus on near term profitability – had not become a factor. Moreover, nearly all employees expected to have their job for life, making the long-term prosperity of the company, and their position within it, much more important than near term remuneration.

INDUSTRIAL CONGLOMERATES

As the once enormous British Empire was dissembled after the Second World War, a new type of empire was born, in the form of industrial conglomerates. Whether publicly listed or privately owned, these corporate behemoths sought to be all things to all people, leveraging corporate infrastructure, financial resources and management skill to build corporate empires that rivalled the political empires of the past.

All of this took place against the long post war economic recovery, a period of moderate growth and generally benign economic conditions. Standards of living improved dramatically, with the advent of simple domestic appliances such as electric cookers, refrigerators, washing machines, radio and television. This, combined with the reassurance of a newly introduced welfare state that promised lifetime healthcare and Government pensions for all in old age, offered a level of security that the ordinary working person had never seen before.

One feature of the 1950s and 1960s was an environment that combined relatively low interest rates and volatile stock-market conditions. Unsurprisingly, this led to the emergence of a raft of conglomerates. These companies bought up a diverse range of businesses, exploiting the gyrations of the stock markets of the day to acquire businesses cheaply, financing the acquisitions with relatively cheap debt. Although there was little or no commercial logic in combining the organisations in question, low financing costs meant that they were able to report increasing earnings year by year.

The growth of these companies was motivated as much by prestige and influence as it was by profit. Their Boards and senior managers were drawn from the upper end of the social spectrum, privately schooled and university educated at institutions such as Oxford and Cambridge in the UK, and Harvard, Princeton and Yale in the US. Promotion was based on personal connections and tenure: if you were a good chap, and had simply been there long enough, you got the next promotion, and you were safe in the knowledge that you had a job for life. Any many of these companies were family fiefdoms, even long after the companies had listed and taken on external shareholders. External relationships were similarly restricted, with the same merchant bank and same law firm likely to be retained as advisors for decades at a time.

Unsurprisingly, these empires sought to spread their risks by diversifying their activities. Whilst logical for the corporation as a whole (and its Board and management), shareholders could achieve such diversification directly through investment strategy. And although many conglomerates have argued that they have fundamental management skills and capabilities that can be leveraged across any business, in practice extremely few have any demonstrable track record of success.

Enter Modigliani and Miller

Meanwhile, in 1958 Modigliani and Miller published their seminal essay, "The Cost of Capital, Corporation Finance and the Theory of Investment" in the American Economic Review. However, although their names are probably the most well known amongst the investment banking community around the world, the birth of economic rationalism had started much earlier. In the 19th century, Karl Marx had written about "fictitious capital", saying:

"The forming of a fictitious capital is called capitalising. Every periodically repeated income is capitalised by calculating it on the average rate of interest, as an income which would be realised by a capital at this rate of interest."

In 1907, the concepts of net present value (and hence discounted cash flow valuation methodologies) were formalised by Irving Fisher in "The rate of Interest". In 1938, John Burr Williams published his "Theory of investment value" and the rather better known Gordon growth model was published by Myron Gordon and Eli Shapiro 1956. What may seem amazing in hindsight is that Fisher's work was not incorporated into academic courses until the 1950s.

These important works gave rise to a whole new class of financial analysis and assessment. In particular, Modigliani and Miller had put forward the idea that the value of a corporation was essentially independent of its capital structure. Over time, this led to a dramatic change in approach, with companies shifting from a focus on maximising profit to one that was driven by maximising their value.

Meanwhile, as interest rates began to rise in response to increasing inflation, the 1950s conglomerates found that underlying companies were unable to increase their profitability sufficiently rapidly. Over time they were forced to restructure and many disappeared.

THE LOST DECADE

In 1970, the top ten companies amongst the Fortune 500 ranked by revenue included four oil & gas majors, three motor vehicle manufacturers, two industrials and one technology company. Despite the warnings inherent in "Limits to Growth", surprisingly little has changed in this group. It still includes three oil & gas companies and two motor vehicle manufacturers, and Apple has replaced IBM as the sole representative of the technology sector.

Nevertheless a great deal has happened in the intervening period. In 1970, US oil production peaked. Indeed, after a brief recovery in the early 1980s, the production of conventional oil has continued to decline ever since. It has more or less halved to levels last seen in the 1950s, over which time the US population has doubled. Meanwhile, in more recent times, there has been an explosion in shale oil and gas production.

In 1971 the US abandoned the gold standard, and other major Western nations followed suit, and most of these countries expanded reserves (printed money) substantially. Oil producing nations in OPEC responded by pinning the oil price to the price of gold, which led to dramatic increases in the oil price, with significant knock-on effects for many economies.

More broadly, major economies struggled with a significant period of high inflation. In the US, the Federal Reserve pursued a high interest rate strategy to attempt to curb inflation. In 1979, the sudden doubling of interest rates led to the savings and loans crisis. Many institutions were impacted, and in the end some 747 of the 3,234 savings and loan associations in the US failed.

Meanwhile in the 1960s and 1970s many Latin American countries had borrowed significant sums of money from American and European banks, in order to finance a period of rapid industrialisation. Petroleum exporting countries had deposited much of their profits in international banks, which had in turn recycled the capital as loans to countries such as Brazil, Argentina and Mexico. When European and US interest rates leapt in the late 1970s, the countries could not meet the repayments and there were a number of major defaults.

At the same time, the UK slumped into a significant recession, and by 1978 unemployment had reached 1.5 million people. In 1976, the UK had faced the humiliation of seeking a £2.3 billion loan from the International Monetary Fund to help combat rampant inflation, which had peaked at over 25% in 1974 and indeed remained at over 10% for nearly a decade. Industrial relations reached a nadir during the "winter of discontent", which saw widespread strikes by public sector trade unions demanding higher pay rises.

Eventually economic stability began to return in the early 1980s. Thatcher was elected as Britain's Prime Minister in 1979 and began an aggressive reform of the economy on many levels. This included extensive privatisation and deregulation, including a significant opening of financial markets. The US similarly saw a return to much more stable economic conditions. In both countries, significant economic growth was driven by the improved operational efficiency as large industry sectors realised significant scale economies through consolidation. A new age began.

ECONOMIC THEORY FINALLY REACHES THE BOARDROOM

Slowly – very, very slowly – the concepts of financial rationalism made their way into the world of finance and mainstream investment banking. Having graduated from Cambridge University, I started my working life in the late 1980s by qualifying as a chartered accountant. This was a common pathway in the UK at that time – most recruits into "corporate finance" as M&A was then known were recently qualified accountants or lawyers.

As a kid, I'd watched my father run a series of large businesses and had developed a fascination not just for how businesses worked, but with why some were able to see and seize opportunities where others could not. One example that still resonates is the birth of television advertising in Saudi Arabia, where we lived in the late 1970s and early 1980s. At that time, television advertising was banned. So if you were trying to launch a new consumer brand, this presented a real challenge (my dad had been hired as the first general manager of Savola, now one of Saudi's largest listed companies). Now Saudi's loved soccer, and UK premier league games were shown in prime time several hours a week. These were, of course, advertising free. But there was nothing stopping you from buying the display advertising behind the goal at Anfield or Old Trafford and filling it with a Saudi brand. Bingo – a heap of prime time TV advertising that otherwise money literally couldn't buy, not to mention the additional credibility to the local viewer of the promotion being associated with some of the UK's premier football clubs. This sowed some critical seeds in my mind about the importance of being prepared to think differently about problems.

So, looking out on the world of employment opportunities in 1989, not long after the 1987 crash, I was lured by the appeal of getting to look under the hood of a whole range of different businesses and understand better how they worked, both commercially and from a financial perspective.

As a result, I saw out the worst of the post crash downturn in the world of accounting, picking up some useful knowledge and bizarre experiences along the way. With the benefit of hindsight, the strangest of these was finding myself, age 24, responsible for designing and implementing the "good bank/bad bank" restructuring of Nordbanken in the UK. The bad assets had all been placed into a UK banking entity shortly before the Christmas holidays, so when we arrived to audit the bank in early January, the December year end had passed.

It was immediately apparent that large write-downs would be required, and that the bank in question would need to be properly recapitalised. If not, a qualified audit opinion was a certainty, and the Bank of England would step in and close the bank down – not at all what the Swedish Government had in mind. The latter was, of course, unthinkable, giving the audit team an unusual degree of leverage to drive through decisions that would impact the future of the business.

So, without a restructuring specialist or investment banker in sight, I led a small team through a rather challenging credit and financing assessment, doing our best to assess when the underlying properties would ever be let, and businesses would ever turn a profit. From this we were able to estimate the likely cost of holding the assets until they reached sustainable levels of income, and hence determine how much capital was required. Armed with this information, we then in turn forced the recapitalisation of the bank, insisting on seeing the funds arrive before the audit was signed off. All of this was achieved in six rather short weeks, and with surprisingly little drama.

The lesson, of course, was an important one. Once again, if you were prepared to think differently, you might just be able to find a solution to what would otherwise be a very challenging problem. Happily I was young enough not to think "no-one has ever done a good bank/bad bank separation in the UK before". We set aside the original approach we might have planned for the audit, and instead put together what was essentially a work-out and refinancing plan for a complex and seriously degraded portfolio. With the benefit of hindsight, this worked well. Further funding was not required, the assets were worked out, and modest profits were realised. In due course, Nordbanken (the good bank) was privatised once again and Securum (the bad bank) was wound up, having fulfilled its purpose.

Later that year, I concluded that I really did want to work in financial services proper, and that if I was to do that I absolutely had to work in the front office. The choice of M&A was easy, as I loved the commercial and long term strategic elements of the role, and had little interest in the second by second activities on the trading floor. I met with many well-known merchant banking businesses (nearly all of which have now disappeared...) and eventually chose to join Barings. The business had a rich history, and had had its ups and downs over the previous 200 years. At its high points, it had once been considered as powerful as major European nations, and had financed America's purchase of Louisiana via a bond issue. The low points included two near failures, as well as several periods of sustained low performance. More than anything, I was drawn by a relatively youthful, focussed and creative new generation of senior bankers, and I was not disappointed.

I arrived at Barings on 10th January 1994 and was immediately thrown into the deep end of corporate finance, M&A and decision-making at some of the UK's largest companies. At that time, most valuations were based almost entirely on looking at simple measures of profit and return – PE multiple and dividend yields. New-fangled concepts of "EV/EBITDA" were making their way across the Atlantic, and the more enterprising bankers were beginning to make use of discounted cash flow models. Of course the previous five years – since the 1987 stock market crash – had been rather quiet, but M&A activity was just about to explode. Between signing and starting, Barings' client Lloyds Bank announced the acquisition of Cheltenham & Gloucester Building Society, then one of the largest acquisitions of a banking entity in the UK of all time. In my first year, a number of other major transactions followed, including the acquisition of TSB, another listed banking entity, which was even larger than Cheltenham and Gloucester. The start of 1995 was marked by a £9 billion hostile bid for our client Wellcome, in what became the largest ever hostile bid to succeed in British history.

Unsurprisingly, Boards were made nervous by the size and complexity of these transactions, and to address this we used more and more sophisticated analysis. In parallel with others in the industry globally, I developed new variants on discounted cash flow models that were better suited to use in highly leveraged, highly regulated entities such as banks and insurers, as well as for utility companies and other businesses subject to more complex constraints where simple cash flow models couldn't be used. We grappled with the challenges of these models, tearing apart the theories and testing the intellectual architecture on which the valuation approaches were built. Most importantly, we understood the need to build financial projections that ran at least ten years into the future. If you didn't, the effects of discounting meant that your valuation was little more than a set of old-fashioned PE multiples.

So it was, some 85 years after Fisher's original paper that began to describe new tools for financial decision-making, that the power of his theories was finally being properly utilised in the world's two major financial markets, the US and the UK. The age of financial rationalism was finally born.

THE SIREN CALL OF COMPOUND GROWTH

Before we look at the impacts of this new belief system, spare a thought for those other soothsayers of the 1970s, the authors of the seminal work "Limits to Growth". Published in 1972 under commission from the Club of Rome, the authors used computer modelling to explore the potential interactions between human population growth and the world's ecosystems. In the book, Donella Meadows, Dennis Meadows, Jorgen Randers and William Behrens III explored the potential inter-relationships between world population, industrialisation, pollution, food production and resource depletion.

At its simplest, the book drew out very clearly that the world has simple, physical system limits which determine the population that it can support. With global population growing exponentially at between 1.5% and 2% a year, the world was set for a dramatic increase in population, which the underlying systems simply couldn't sustain. Growth rates at this level sound low compared to the growth achieved in corporate profits over recent decades. Over longer time periods, however, they imply dramatic increases – 2% growth for a hundred years implies seven-fold growth.

Imagine if this had happened in New York? In 1900, the population was around 3.4 million. If the population had grown at 2% a year, by 2010 it would have reached just over 30 million (in fact it was just 8.2 million). Of course you might think that this is unsurprising, and that the growth would be easier to accommodate outside the big cities. If this had happened, then the 1900 US population of 76.2 million people would have reached 673 million in 2010. With infrastructure already under pressure in North America, imagine what challenges this would bring.

Much of the original analysis in "Limits to Growth" has stood the test of the last 50 years remarkably well. This is, of course, a warning bell for much of the industrialised world, as the book illustrates clearly that practical system limits on the world mean that rapidly increasing population will create substantial challenges in many areas. Of these, the impact of greenhouse gases such as carbon dioxide on the world's climate is probably the most talked about. Its effects have already been significant, not just in terms of increases in average temperatures, but also as seen in other very measurable factors such as loss of Arctic ice. Minimum summer ice cover of the Arctic has fallen 50% or so since 1970, and indeed summer ice volumes have fallen around 75%, meaning that an ice-free Arctic in the summer now appears quite possible with a decade or two.

Perhaps one of the most important messages inherent within "Limits to Growth" was the suggestion that we should be very wary of factoring in significant real growth over long time periods. Whilst economic growth of 3% to 4% a year (and more in the case of China) may be sustainable over the near term, when judged over 100 year periods such growth is unlikely to be achieved, as it just won't prove unsustainable in practice. Thus as companies are setting strategies and Governments are determining policy, it is critical that they beware the siren call of compound growth.

BUSINESS SCHOOLS AND THE BIRTH OF FINANCIAL RATIONALISM

For thirty years or more, business thinking in the Western world has been driven by financial rationalism. Born in the (almost exclusively American) business schools of the 1970s and 1980s, proponents argued for corporate decisions to be made based on "objective financial analysis". In practice, this meant rigorous determination of future cash flows, not just business profits. It also called for "proper" consideration to be given to the time value of money, through the use of discounted cash flow appraisal techniques.

This revolution of business decision-making was radical and went hand in hand with a variety of welcome developments, including a move towards merit based promotion, increased diversity and a slow reduction in recruitment based on old school tie connections. The twin comfort blankets of jobs for life and "Buggin's turn" promotions were abolished in favour of a new meritocracy, with the universal effectiveness of the free market as its mantra.

Business decision-making moved on from simple profit maximisation to a new focus on maximising the value of the company as a whole, promoted by optimal capital structures and measured by discounted cash flow valuations. In the excitement of this new order, the acolytes in business schools and corporate boardrooms appear to have forgotten the health warning that should, in retrospect, have been printed in 100 point type on every financial text book over the last thirty years:

"If you're going to discount everything, discount your valuation model too!"

Unconstrained by this health warning, and armed with new tools to appraise corporate initiatives, infrastructure projects, investments in healthcare and prospective new technologies, a whole generation of managerial bureaucrats was unleashed with an open license to drive corporate and capital efficiency and, most importantly, "shareholder value".

They began with dismantling the remaining multi-national conglomerates whose activities spanned diverse industries and markets. These organisations were, in turn, largely the failed by-product of an experiment in the benefits of diversification. Multi-industry, multi-national behemoths ruled the world stage for a time, at least until investors realised that, with efficient and liquid stock exchanges, they could construct these businesses themselves in investment portfolios. Of course these stock exchanges had been around for 100 years or more, so why it took so long to write-off the conglomerate business model remains a mystery. The new world asset strippers ripped apart these edifices of corporate excess. Bankers supplied what then appeared to be mountains of debt, and the perpetrators were incentivised by a significant share in the upside. Indeed, simply by stripping out layer upon layer of expensive central management cost, and selling the occasional non-core subsidiary, much value could be created.

As the new mantra of financial rationalism took hold, a new breed of corporate raider was born. Armed with a newfound ability to apply huge leverage to ailing corporate empires, asset strippers and their new-found investment banking friends acquired aging companies, dissected them and sold their body parts to their competitors, and paid down borrowings as rapidly as possible. Huge value was unlocked by bringing new rigour to the management of companies, inspired by a focus on cash flows, business focus and capital structure optimisation, not to mention hefty financial incentives for management. Investors who backed these leveraged buyouts expected and received annualised returns on equity of 40% a year or more, dramatically better than returns on equity over the previous hundred years or more.

Meanwhile, aging corporations that were not so badly inflicted with the supremacy gene saw the writing on the wall and sold off non-core activities, exited unprofitable markets, and joined the refrain of focus and specialisation. Even Governments joined the bandwagon, recognising that politicians and bureaucrats were not necessarily the best managers of companies that provided mined petroleum, or provided electricity, or ran the water and sewage system or provided telephone services.

Slowly and subtly, many people were drawn in to the focus on shareholder value, and how best to increase shareholder value rapidly. In the 1990s, corporations began to promise a doubling of shareholder value every five years, then every four, and finally every three. The last implies compound growth in valuation of 26% a year, and even the first implies growth of some 15% a year compound. Clearly these figures could never be achieved other than in the very short term. Indeed even companies such as Google, which has an extraordinary track record and started from a low base, struggle to achieve such figures for more than a decade.

Unsurprisingly, then, a new style of corporate survival of the fittest played out in the 1990s. Some of the most successful companies were those which were adept at acquiring their competitors, whether through all share transactions or taking on even higher levels of leverage. Some of the biggest beneficiaries of this were the CEOs and top management themselves. Remuneration experts devised yet more complex incentive structures, repeating week by week the mantra of "better alignment with shareholder interests". CEO compensation increased dramatically. Market indices rocketed and share prices of many organisations reached record high after record high.

To add to this heady mix, the internet boom emerged in the mid 1990s. Early progress was relatively slow, held back by the incredibly slow data rates provided by 28k and 56k modems. Once ADSL technology became widely available to consumers in the year 2000, the pace of development began to accelerate, and by 2004 Google had listed at an offering price of $85 a share, giving it a market capitalisation of $23bn. Since then the stock has risen more than ten-fold, making for a compound rate of return of over 30%.

FINANCIAL WARLORDS

But for every Google, there have been numerous other companies brought to market with spectacular stories that singularly failed to deliver. Indeed one of the most striking features of the period from 1995 to the financial crisis in 2007 was the dramatic increase in the power and reach of the global investment banks. Most of these organisations had once been private stock companies or partnerships, with the bank's capital owned directly by the senior partners. During the 1980s and 1990s, however, most had become listed public companies, allowing retiring partners to monetise their significant investments in the firm, and new partners to leverage the firm's capital with substantial outside investment.

And leverage they did, both in terms of their own capital structures, and in how they packaged and redistributed risk to maximise their own short term profitability. They assembled massive global teams, and a number were acquired and backed by some of the world's largest banking entities.

These were the financial warlords of their time, supported by armies of investment bankers numbering in the tens of thousands. They acquired most of the remaining European merchant banks, and established leading positions in every major market in the world. By 2000, investment banking was dominated globally by around eight to ten firms. They provided capital and dealing limits and liquidity wherever it was required, positioning themselves as the universal counterparties to almost any trade. With credit terms becoming looser and looser, and financial models apparently becoming more and more sophisticated, they were able to achieve massive leverage on their already expanded capital bases and take enormous positions, both directly and through the extensive use of derivatives.

This activity, not to mention the frenetic excitement of investors and investment managers around the world, stoked a dramatic equity and debt bubble the like of which the world has never seen before. Meanwhile the investment bankers had taken their own medicine, not just driving for increases in profit, but stretching their capital structures as far as possible to maximise the value of all activity not just of the firm, but for the people that controlled the firm.

Governments too loaded up on cheap debt, using it to maintain state sector employment and pay for welfare benefits and allowing state spending to grow significantly more rapidly than the tax base. In some cases this has gone significantly beyond what the countries can realistically afford, resulting in a substantial wealth transfer from future generations (who will bear the burden of interest on the debt) to the present generation.

Bang.

Eventually this bubble had to explode, which it did in dramatic style starting in 2007 and continuing for several years. The after-effects are recent history and need no repeating here. Suffice it to say that many countries have gone through a painful period of adjustment, and indeed many still are. The corporate sector has had a somewhat easier time, in relative terms at least, but some industries (including investment banking) have seen a dramatic reduction in their workforces.

WHERE TO FROM HERE?

The events of the last decade hold incredibly important lessons. With the pace of change in many industries continuing to accelerate, and the painful lessons of recent years fresh in the corporate pysche, now is the time to look long and hard at our collective faith in the principals of financial rationalism.

We need to start by remembering the basic principal that a company's value is driven by its fundamental profitability and prospects. This value is, of course, only realised over time, much of it over the longer term. Five years of success may return only 15% to 20% of the value in the form of dividends to shareholders, and much less than that in a high growth company. So we have to focus on maximising the profits that the company can achieve over the long term – ie ten years or more.

Even more importantly, the last decade has seen unprecedented change in many industries. This pace of that change continues to accelerate, meaning that we can be less and less certain about what the future will hold. This presents a fundamental challenge for conventional cash flow based valuations, which require a level of certainty in the base case forecasts to be able to generate meaningful valuations. This in turn highlights the importance of judging performance by metrics that are likely to drive success over the longer term, and not simply the most recent quarter's profit. If you doubt this for a second, remember the relative fortunes of Nokia and Apple over the last decade.

Just as we moved from a focus on profit to a focus on the value of an organisation, we must now leave behind the age of financial rationalism and find a new, more robust set of principals to guide corporate and Government decision-making. We must bury financial rationalism, which has driven us to focus on value as an instantaneous data point and look beyond this to focus on when and how that value can be unlocked in the form of profits over time.

8. You've escaped, so don't look back!

WELCOME TO THE ACCIDENTAL PRESENT

So you are ready to start rebuilding your business, or indeed you might be considering building a new one. You're thinking about the longer term, not just the next quarterly report. You want to create a growing stream of profits, not just achieve a short term jump in your stock price. And you are starting to figure out flaws with the internal structure of your organisation as well as market barriers that you may have to break down. You're starting to look at the entire ecosystem around you in new ways.

Before you go too far, you should pause and reflect on where your business is today. Why does it offer the particular range of products or services currently shown on the web site? Why does it have a presence in some regions and not in others. For international businesses, why do you have a different mix of products and services in overseas markets compared to your home country. And what is the strategic rationale behind the operational or management structure currently employed. Were any of these things the result of long term planning, or were there other factors at work?

Stop and ask the question: does anyone know why we are here? Take mobile phones and the current obsession with apps. Apple fought to differentiate its devices and their unique operating system on the basis that they had more apps than anyone else. In practice, Google's Android was able to catch up very quickly, and even Blackberry and Microsoft are nowhere near as far behind as they once were.

But looking at the bigger picture, does this even matter? Apps were born following the advent of smart phones (ie very small, mobile computers that can also make phone calls) connected to 3G wireless data networks. The phones' processing power was modest. This made it impossible to run full computer programmes that offered a slick interface and real-time interactivity. In addition, these phones connected to networks that had very limited bandwidth and the charges for data were high. The solution was to put most of the functionality into a very small, cut-down application on the phone, and then call limited amounts of real time data in small, quick-to-download packets from central servers. The app was born. Importantly, it wasn't the best possible solution imaginable – it was simply the best one that worked within the constraints of the time and the technology then available.

But 4G connections offer much faster data connections – similar to or better than ADSL 2 fixed line internet speeds – and wifi networks are slowly but surely becoming ubiquitous in urban areas at least. And the processing power of smart-phone chips is more or less the same as found in laptop computers of just a couple of years ago. So the need for apps installed on mobile devices is rapidly diminishing for many services and innovations as web languages such as HTML 5 open up the potential for a whole new approach. This will be much more effective than the app in many niches, not least because there is no need to download the app in advance, allowing owners of the services to stay out of the clutches of individual app stores.

So much of our world is co-incidence and accident, born of historic circumstances and the needs and choices of a previous time. Much of the time we take the results of these choices for granted, with no thought for whether or not they represent the best choice for the present circumstances.

Did you ever stop to wonder why so many of the world's capital cities are located on rivers? Or how many major coastal cities are on major river estuaries? Today we take safe harbours and fresh water for granted, but it wasn't always so.

Why did Columbus sail to the Caribbean? In the 15th Century, once you left the coastline behind, you could only reliably sail East or West. Travelling North or South was fraught with navigational danger, as clocks weren't accurate enough to allow you to navigate precisely. So, Columbus sailed South along the coast of Europe and Africa, to the well-established port on Gran Canaria in the Canary Islands. From there, he followed the trade winds west to see what he could find. After a five week journey, the expedition spotted land, a small Caribbean island now called San Salvador, discovered for no other reason than it lay more or less due west of the starting point.

Similarly, have you ever wondered why anyone ever sailed to Fremantle all those years ago? It's now a small, vibrant port on the vast West coast of Australia. In the early 17th Century, a series of Dutch voyagers explored the south Pacific. With no Suez Canal, the only way to get there was to follow Southwards in the footsteps of Columbus, continuing to the very bottom of South Africa and around the Cape of Good Hope. From there, having replenished supplies at Port Elizabeth or Durban, you sailed due East, hoping to find land (the trade winds blow East in the southern hemisphere).

Indeed as early as 1504, the French navigator Binot Paulmier de Gonneville claimed to have landed at a land east of the Cape of

Good Hope, having being blown off course, although this was eventually shown to be Brazil, not Australia. Other explorers made a truer course, arriving at Fremantle and Perth, located at two river estuaries that offer a safe harbour and fresh water for seafarers.

In both examples, the travellers simply arrived at the best ports (indeed more or less the only ports) that you find if you follow the trade winds West or East from the original ports of departure. So each of these destinations were very much an accident of where the great explorers of the day had started their journeys. Even that starting point was an accident, lying on the coast South from the home ports of the explorers in question.

BLOWING WITH THE CORPORATE WINDS OF DESTINY

How often is this true of companies? How many organisations have inherited a legacy of market position, business model and strategy which is an accident of the past? Think about airlines for a moment. The world's great airlines of the post war era were located at the end of the world's major air routes, many of which emanated from the UK in the dying days of the British Empire. British Overseas Airways Corporation and British Caledonian operated romantic long distance routes in the 1950s and 1960s that stopped in locations now hardly visited at all by long haul travellers. As a child, I lived in Bahrain, once one of three or four stops on the all-important long distance journey to Australia. Bahrain was then a vibrant meeting point, visited by travellers from many nations travelling East and West.

Then, in 1970, the 747 was born. This was the world's first wide body jet, and has remained in service ever since. At the time, Boeing thought that only around 400 would be sold before the aircraft was made obsolete by the advent of wide-spread supersonic travel. In practice, over 1,400 have been built, and the "jumbo jet" has been in commercial production for over 40 years.

The first variant, the 747-100, had a range of 9,800 kilometres, just long enough to fly from London directly to Bangkok. In 1975, the 747 SP was introduced, with a range extended to 10,840 kilometres with a full load of 331 passengers, and significantly more with lighter payloads. This allowed non-stop flights between London and Hong Kong (remembering that in those days Russian airspace was closed, necessitating much longer routes over India and the Middle East).

Bahrain's role in long haul international travel ended almost overnight – it was no longer needed as a staging post on the way to Asia. Ironically, in the modern world, jets with ranges of 15 flying hours or more now mean that you can fly direct from the Middle East to nearly everywhere, and airlines such as Emirates have capitalised on their location as a global hub, opening up direct routes from Dubai to places as far away as San Francisco and Sydney. But Bahrain has never recovered its place as one of the world's major air hubs.

Australia's own national champion, Qantas, was once at the terminus for one of the world's key air journeys, the Kangaroo route from Sydney to London. But in an environment where the winners are located at the hubs of long distance travel, Qantas now suffers from being at the end of a long spoke that leads to nowhere but regional Australia and New Zealand.

How can Qantas ever build a successful long haul airline, when it only naturally serves a local customer base of some 25 million people, compared to the 6 billion reached by Emirates or Etihad? By its own admission, it needs to start from somewhere else and is exploring new hubs in Asia. But then what does it bring to those hubs and consumers in those countries? It has to pack its corporate bags, get on its own long haul flight, and set up in an entirely new market, serving entirely new customers, armed only with its experiences and impeccable safety record. Make no mistake, Qantas may achieve this, but to embark on this journey requires a level of corporate bravery rarely seen in today's global leaders. Meanwhile, it has partnered with Emirates from Dubai, effectively exiting from the routes to Europe, opening up the possibility to focus more on a more diverse Asian route network and leaving behind nearly a century of corporate history.

DISRUPTIVE INNOVATION OR PREDICTABLE CHANGE?

The good news is that the nature of the seismic changes in technology that have driven radical reshaping of industries have frequently been entirely predictable. It was inevitable, for example, that aircraft ranges would increase over time. All you need is a world globe and a measure of distance to see which journeys become possible. Armed with a basic understanding of the world's business activity and demographics, you can start to think quite deeply about what such changes may mean for incumbents and their business models.

The same is true of the advent of smart phones. Over the last thirty years, computers have been miniaturised, the resolution of small screens has increased significantly and battery technologies have improved steadily. So it was only a matter of time before the smart phone – a small mobile computer with telephony added in – became a reality. Indeed, if you had tracked the development of technology, you could also have predicted the timing quite accurately. Meanwhile radio transmission technology and associated bandwidth availability has also increased quite predictably from the first digital networks in the early 1990s, to 3G a decade later and 4G today.

There are also natural barriers to further development. For air travel, the dramatically increased fuel costs, as well as noise impacts of supersonic travel, have meant that the Concorde technology that was first developed in the 1960s never saw significant commercial deployment. Meanwhile in mobile communication, 4G data transmission is now operating close to physical limits, making further advances unlikely. Similarly ADSL 2+ operates at the physical limits of a copper network. This means that any further material increases in bandwidth requirements will need to be met by the deployment of fibre networks, where the physical constraints allow massively greater bandwidth.

Look at the types of innovation that are entirely predictable today. Computing power will continue to increase, power use will fall and miniaturisation will continue. Desktop PCs have already begun to disappear into slightly chunkier display screens, and before long an oversized iPad will be all you see on the desk, albeit likely still accompanied by a keyboard as these remain much more efficient for inputting data than touch screens.

There will be a revolution in the sources of energy. Hydrocarbon fuelled power stations will disappear, along with the associated pollution, and will be replaced by cheaper, zero emission renewable energy sources.

Meanwhile existing patents already point to medical devices the size of a USB key that could diagnose hundreds of diseases in minutes, rather than days. Shrinking this type of equipment will dramatically reduce costs, as the most expensive components –

specialist chemical reagents – will only be required in picolitre quantities. Even the chips will become cheaper, reduced in size so that hundreds or thousands can be manufactured on a single wafer. If this sounds fanciful, remember than dozens of universities have teams specialising in micro-electrical mechanical systems and micro-fluidics, and there are at least half a dozen organisations globally with hundreds of patents in related fields, all seeking to develop technology which would revolutionise the cost and availability of this type of healthcare.

These changes will each drive dramatic changes in whole industries. And as they say in stock-market investing, the past is not necessarily any guide to the future. The way that industries have operated and profits made may bear absolutely no relationship to the new business paradigms that emerge.

How clear is the crystal ball?

How many record labels rejected The Beatles? How many publishers said 'no' to Harry Potter? If the next Facebook walked into the Facebook boardroom, would Mark Zuckerburg and colleagues invest in the new pretender? Or would they think that the company was simply too speculative, too different, too risky? Remember, eight years later the original Facebook listed at a $100 billion valuation, having added an average of over 300,000 monthly active users a day since its launch in 2004. Revolutionary successes are by definition easy to see in hindsight, but how do you spot a business that will define a generation before it becomes great?

Around the world, opportunities for dramatic and revolutionary change walk in and out of meeting rooms every day. Projects that offer a billion dollars of upside opportunity, with genuinely limited downside risks, are quietly rejected. Often the risks appear too great, or the vision is too far removed from where the perceived opportunities lie. Meanwhile, some CEOs and leadership teams are being criticised for a lack of boldness. With the benefit of hindsight, some business decisions that maintained the status quo have destroyed tens of billions of dollars of value. But, over the near term, evolution feels much safer than revolution.

There are, of course, many ideas that succeeded in attracting investment, and then have slipped quietly into history without leaving any legacy. But how many truly great ideas or businesses or stories or bands have gone undiscovered, because they were too new, too different, or too far ahead of their time to resonate with those who had the opportunity to support them? The Fab Four, JK Rowling and Walt Disney all succeeded despite great scepticism, but this was down to a very small number of individuals who decided to back their judgement and try something completely new.

Meanwhile, companies sometimes talk about reinventing or future-proofing their businesses as they try to adapt to the digital, more social age. In practice, some seem to struggle to reinvent even their logos. This is a harsh caricature, but what does it really take to deliver true innovation, to invent something genuinely new, that captures hearts and minds and wallets? Over the centuries, many major industries have been turned on their heads by radical innovations. Examples include cars replacing horses, computers replacing ledger clerks and smart phones replacing analogue phones. As a result, new industry leaders have been born and old industries have been wiped out in a matter of years. Indeed the pace of change is accelerating, so spotting these changes and opportunities is critical for any large company.

Over the next twenty years, the most successful businesses will be those that can adapt best to a world that is changing more and more rapidly. Many will be transfixed by the confusion of uncertainty regarding the nature and timing of game changing developments. Corporate rabbits in the headlights, they will stand watching, entirely mesmerised as a new technology arrives and flattens their business. There are already plenty of real world examples and so I will not name names here. For innovators, the good news is that large corporations that have the potential to be fearsome competitors may allow you the time and freedom of movement you need to succeed. Vested interests – and no doubt the supremacy gene – hold these potential competitors back.

Let's take a step back for a moment. You will be familiar with Moore's law, which says that the number of transistors on integrated circuits will double every two years. First identified in 1965, Gordon Moore predicted that this trend would last for at least ten years. In recent times, the logic has almost been turned on its head, with semi-conductor companies having used the law as a target to drive ongoing research and development.

A similar pattern applies to the predictability of the future. Think about the great revolutions of the last 1,000 years. By greatest, I mean those innovations that had the most profound impact on health, safety and the quality of life.

The first five hundred years of the second millennium saw the development of gunpowder, banking (in Italy in the 14th Century), printing (in Germany in 1440), as well as significant improvements in shipbuilding, enabling explorers to discover the new world. It also saw the renaissance, and in particular the rediscovery and redeployment of many Roman and Greek technologies.

The next 250 years, from 1500 to 1750, were marked by the agricultural which transformed agricultural production through the use of modern crop rotation, as well as the beginnings of the industrial revolution, which triggered significant economic growth through the automation and efficiency of factories. Significant advances were also made in optics (the invention of the telescope), Newton discovered gravity and William Gilbert began to understand electricity.

In the next 150 years, a number of key aspects of the modern world were first invented. These include the telegraph (in the early 1800s), the telephone (1875), the first gasoline powered motor car (1885), the discovery of antibiotics (1887) and the radio (1895).

By 1900, the pace of invention had accelerated dramatically. That year the zeppelin was invented, as was the first modern escalator. The safety razor and vacuum cleaner followed in 1901. In 1902 the air conditioner was invented, along with the neon light. The first aeroplane flew in 1903 and the vacuum diode was created in 1904. Albert Einstein published his theory of relativity in 1905. The Model T Ford was first sold in 1908 and by 1910 the first talking motion picture was shown. In 1913 the modern zipper was invented and by 1919 the world had short wave radio. Insulin was invented in 1922 and the first 3D movie was shown. Cathode ray tubes, the self-winding watch and frozen food followed the next year. Spiral binding was created in 1924 and the television followed in 1925.

The next 25 years included technicolor, the aerosol can, the iron lung, penicillin, the analog computer, the jet engine, the electron microscope, zoom lenses, radio telescopes, FM radio, stereo records, cats eyes, tape recorders, nylon, radar, photocopiers, ballpoint pens, LSD, teflon, freeze dried coffee, colour television, the neutronic reactor, digital computers, the aqualung, kidney dialysis, the atomic bomb, microwave ovens and velcro.

Many of the inventions from the first half of the twentieth century are things that we take entirely for granted today – although in some cases it is surprising how long ago they were first conceived. The second half of the twentieth century has seen even more remarkable developments in agricultural science, medicine, computers, technology, optics and others. Meanwhile previous inventions have been significantly refined, becoming smaller, cheaper, more effective and more reliable. Indeed the last fifty years have seen so many inventions of fundamental importance to everyday life, health and welfare that it is meaningless to try to pick the most significant. They include nuclear power, the personal computer, mobile phones, the internet and much more beyond.

Meanwhile the last ten years has seen the emergence of online and technology behemoths – Google, Facebook and Apple, each of which has created entire new business ecosystems.

In the year 1000, the future was much more predictable than it is today. Indeed, very little changed in the world over the first 200 years of the second millennium. Even over the first five hundred years, most of the inventions represented relatively modest improvements to existing technologies. Probably the most dramatic advances, in Northern Europe at least, came about through the rediscovery of 1,000 year old technologies that had been in widespread use in the Roman and Greek empires.

Compare this to the last hundred years. How many of the inventions of the last decade could have been predicted at the start of the twentieth century? Some parts of our lives are almost entirely unchanged – we still eat more or less exactly the same types of meats and fruits and vegetables as our great grandparents. Availability and cost may have changed, and we have moved back to organic produce, but much is little different from a hundred years ago. Meanwhile there has been dramatic, but nevertheless predictable, improvement in the new technologies of that time. This includes motor cars, telephones, air travel and many similar things. In other areas, however, there have been inventions that were unthinkable just a few generations ago.

In truth, even for much of the last forty years, there have been many things that have changed little on a decadal view. Fixed line telephones still work the same way that they did in the 1980s. Broadcast television has finally been upgraded to high definition, the first change since the 1970s, and colour resolutions have improved. Cars still use petrol, and are only 50% to 100% more efficient than in my childhood (compare that to computers). Electricity networks around the world still largely use 110V and 220V AC. The Boeing 747 is still one of the world's most used commercial airliners.

Indeed, in some areas we have gone backwards. Man no longer goes to the moon, and indeed the world's fastest commercial airliner is no longer Concorde (first test flown in 1969). Many countries are struggling to finance the rebuilding of aging infrastructure, and many countries run train services that are slower today than in the age of steam. Even in technology, Nokia has only just been surpassed as the vendor of the most mobile phone handsets after more than a decade in the top spot, and the large majority of the world's documents are still written using Microsoft Word.

But there have also been more and more inventions that were unthinkable. So what do we look for in this uncertain world?

SWITCHING ON THE INNOVATION RADAR

Let's start with predictable innovation. Some future developments are arguably quite predictable if you know what metrics to consider. Although the innovation and design along the way have been wonderful for consumers, the advent of the modern smart-phone itself should be no surprise. At the simplest level, this represents the logical outcome of the miniaturisation of computers, the evolution of touch screens, optimisation of data transmission in the microwave range and improving battery life. None of these developments have been particularly surprising, and indeed even the timing of progress was relatively clear to those who were close to these elements of the technology.

So in short, there are areas where the individual steps are innovative, but the overall result is relatively predictable over time horizons of a decade or more. True innovation in these areas should be relatively easy to find, as it really just represents the realisation of an anticipated product. So you will know what to look for – simply the best realisation of the product in question. In practice, though, to find or create the winners requires a very open mind about what is possible. Steve Jobs is famous for his "reality distortion field", which enabled Apple to hit the mark with the iPhone – combining music, camera, telephone and mobile computing into one superbly designed unit with a slick interface. Or as Steve Jobs said, "Amazing!".

Other innovations are much more challenging to get off the ground – this is the innovators' paradox. In particular, no matter how exciting or innovative a new opportunity appears, and how much hype there is around the business in question, you have to look through the short term euphoria and think carefully about the forces that are at work. How many people or customers will benefit from the technology in question? Will they be prepared to pay for it and thus translate the ideas into customer numbers and growing profits? This highlights the importance of clear, conservative and well thought out plans as to how they will create value and achieve sustainable growth at an early stage.

Whatever the near-term hype, this type of success will be identified in the traditional way. In particular, valuations will be determined by conventional valuation metrics such as enterprise value divided by EBITDA. So you find them by testing carefully how they will generate a profit, how long that will take to achieve, and how their valuation multiples should compare to other companies.

Finally, There are other examples, however, where invention creates entirely new businesses. This type of invention is a truly intriguing process – both elusive and addictive. Like morning light, you know this kind of invention once it is properly established, but the dawning itself is an imperceptible moment in time. Social media has dramatically increased the ease with which people and companies can achieve this kind of success. The viral success of long established Korean singer Psy's "Gangnam style" video, with some 532 million views on YouTube in barely three months, proves this point. Almost unheard of outside Korea before July 2012, his act is now famous worldwide and the video is one of the most viewed of all time.

Social media itself, and the leading companies in the space, are also great examples of meteoric success made valuable in the business world. The appeal or longevity of businesses such as Facebook, Twitter and Pinterest was genuinely hard to predict at the outset, as they offered something entirely new. Indeed this is borne out by Twitter's slow and patchy growth in monthly average users over the first couple of years.

Inertia and the market power of incumbents can weigh heavily against companies like this, even if it does not impact individual artists like Psy. So these types of opportunities are much harder to spot, just as many people turned down The Beatles and JK Rowling.

What does this mean for companies and other large organisations? More than anything, that it is incredibly important to keep an open mind, to be prepared to change your assumptions and beliefs if you are presented with something radically new, and to be prepared to unlearn.

So the pathway to greatness is a highly unpredictable one in many fields. Along the way there are, however, critical points with binary outcomes at which truly innovative ideas will flourish or fail, businesses will succeed or go bust. And all too often, the factors that determine success or failure seem almost random. In the same way that you look carefully both ways before you cross a busy road, entrepreneurs somehow need to sense when these defining moments will be, and to make sure that they are as well prepared as possible. And most importantly, although history will always provide useful context, it is much more important to look forward to what is possible. You need to know where you are going.

9. Never mind the strategy, where are we going?

THE ACCIDENTAL CIRCUMNAVIGATION OF SARK

Imagine you are on a long distance ocean racing yacht, sailing up to the start line for a 5,000 nautical mile leg across one of the world's fiercest oceans. If you ask the captain where you're going, she'll give you the name of the port at the end of the race. She certainly won't tell you that you're on a course of 243 degrees making your way towards a navigation mark. She also won't tell you that you're in a tacking duel with your fiercest competitor to secure the most favourable line to the start. Both these things may be true, but neither of them are your destination.

So it is in business.

Or rather so it should be. Many companies have some kind of aspirational vision – to be the biggest or best in some way or other. Nearly all have strategies for building their businesses and attempting to be more successful than their current closest competitors. And many listed companies are obsessed with the tactical considerations related to the corporate reporting cycle, driving up earnings per share quarter by quarter. But all too few have a clearly enunciated destination. In other words they can't say where they are actually going over the medium to long term. Nor will you necessarily ever know when they have arrived.

And to be clear here, this destination really needs to be a place that is clearly different from where you are now. Simply staying the biggest in a particular market or segment is rarely clear enough to drive an organisation to improve, redefine and renew its core strengths. More likely this approach will encourage the supremacy gene to take hold, setting the business up for long term underperformance. And in a world that is changing more and more rapidly, the status quo is simply not an option. As Groucho Marx famously said: "The problem with doing nothing is that you never know when you're finished".

As an example, think of all the organisations that are targeting "Asian growth". For many, this simply means that they have recognised that economies in Asia are growing more rapidly than economies in Europe and North America, and that they'd like to increase the proportion of profit that they make in the Asia region to differentiate themselves from their peers. But this is not a destination. It's simply an aspirational desire to spend a bit more time in another place where the corporate grass appears to be a little greener.

In practice, Asia isn't a place in its own right – you can't fly to the capital of Asia. More importantly, each country has its own particular characteristics and peculiarities. Each market operates very separately from the others, with different dynamics, different consumer preferences and different factors driving economic and social development. So "Asian growth" is little more than an after dinner craving for something sweet. It isn't a strategy and it certainly isn't a destination.

The concept of strategy is, of course, nothing new. Unsurprisingly, many of the early texts on strategy relate to the building of nations and, in particular, the fighting of wars. Of course in a war the destination is very clear – it is simply to conquer the opponent and win the war, at more or less any cost, with the losers often paying the ultimate price. It is a life or death battle, with few shades of grey. Even a Pyrrhic victory is likely to be preferred by the survivors to dying on the front line.

In business, winning is an illusion. Victory is only ever momentary, reflecting a confluence of factors that combine vision, strategy, skill and luck, not necessarily in equal measure. And as the pace of change continues to accelerate, the latest market darling can become yesterday's hero remarkably quickly. This is especially true if the company becomes over-confident of its market position, its strategy and its capability to deliver. The supremacy gene takes over, and the rot sets in.

It is much the same in government and politics. Although political representatives understandably complain about being caught up in an endless whirl of hourly media reports, and face the acid test of an election every few years, their real success is judged by their legacy of policy achievements.

In the long distance yacht race, the destination is always precisely defined. No matter what the weather, and no matter what the wind direction, the eventual goal is clear to the whole crew. Short term changes in course will be needed, by the minute, hour and day, to reflect changing environmental conditions. But whatever these changes are, the captain and her crew will be working together to ensure that the yacht crosses a finish line that is defined before the race starts.

Businesses and governments need concrete destinations too. Once you mark your destination clearly on the chart, you can be blown off course by the weather, but you will still be able to adjust course and continue to head towards your goal. Without a clear destination, the moment the environment changes, you'll start to wander off course. Each time you meet a new challenge, the navigational choices will seem more and more complicated, and the right choice will be harder and harder to identify.

Before you know it, you'll be lost, confused, and like as not heading for the rocks of accidental destiny.

This happened to me once in real life, aboard a yacht in the English Channel (a Sigma 38 called Steamy Windows, for what it's worth). We left Guernsey to sail for Jersey – an easy day sail of around 30 miles. Our captain had planned the route and called for a south easterly course to be set. Before long, the island appeared, and we began to make our way around to the southern side, where the main port of St Helier lies. But as we did, the compass bearings started to wander from what we expected from the chart. The landmarks didn't quite make sense. Our captain and the crew became more and more confused, not sure whether to trust our collective eyes or the wandering compass. Soon we were travelling at 90 degrees to our original intended course. We knew something was wrong, but we struggled to understand what. We had a strategy – travel South East! But we didn't really know where we going.

The truth is, as we'd left the harbour, we'd never been able to see our destination clearly, nor did the crew really understand precisely where we were going. It was early in my sailing career and I was still learning the basics of navigation – which is particularly challenging in the English channel due to the very strong tidal currents. We needed to sail slightly South of East, and hold that course for at least 20 miles. We shouldn't have expected to see the island in question for at least the first hour, and maybe two. If we knew our true destination, then when we spotted land quite quickly, just a little to the left of its anticipated location, we would have known it was not where we were going. We would have ignored the distraction, and held our course in the Easter sunshine.

In fact, we were accidentally circumnavigating Sark, a much smaller island surrounded by many small, treacherous rocky outcrops. At some point, one of the crew stood back from the noise, trusted the instruments and the chart, and figured out rapidly exactly where we were. Sensibly, we all listened, including the captain (CEOs and Cabinet Ministers please note). Luckily we avoided the disaster of hitting the many submerged reefs – it was March, meaning that the survival time if you ended up in the sea was only minutes. We completed the circumnavigation and headed back to St Peterport, having learned salutary lessons in navigation and leadership. If you don't know where you are going, no amount of strategy, expert captainship or teamwork will get you there.

CORPORATE IDOL WORSHIP

Businesses and governments do not necessarily read the signs that they are off course or heading towards the rocks so easily. Indeed in the heat of the moment, with conflicting information, economic uncertainty and the pressures of the next reporting cycle or election, keeping a clear mind and holding your course can be incredibly hard. So it is important to be mindful of the more obvious traps into which many organisations fall.

Governments and major corporations around the world face many significant challenges day by day. Pretty much every one of these organisations, whether in the private or public sector, has a "too hard" basket, into which it throws many of the really important problems, because there are no easy, obvious or practical solutions. Indeed, the harder and more closely they look at these problems, the more fundamental they seem, and the more challenging they appear to be to solve.

Does this sound familiar? Of course, what is worse is what happens next. We grow to know and love these problems, and the impossible challenges that they represent. We cherish and admire them, burnishing them in the collective corporate psyche as we enunciate ever more clearly just how difficult they are to solve, and how smart we are for understanding the challenges and being able to implement even marginal improvements in the face of them. Before long, there is an organisational trophy cabinet filled with insuperable challenges, each accompanied by its own rich history.

If you could ask George Orwell to write a business sequel to follow his political masterpiece *"1984"*, surely "*1985*" would explore how organisations get sucked into fighting to preserve an entirely undesirable status quo, rather than having the courage to fix the underlying problem once and for all.

This is the worst type of corporate idol worship. You'll know your organisation is suffering from it if, every year or two, a new working group is formed to tackle the same old high priority problems. External consultants are hired to bring "fresh perspective", doubtless further illuminating the tremendous difficulty of ever reaching an attractive solution. Each time, the working group responsibly concludes that the problem is just too big to address in its entirety. Combining this with the supremacy gene makes for a particularly lethal recipe, as the organisation in question will know that it has all the answers. So any staff member or external consultant who comes forward thinking they have a solution clearly just doesn't understand the problem.

Meanwhile, as the years pass, the working groups begin to recognise increasing risk – not in fixing the problem, of course, but rather in implementing the changes needed to address it. This is a subtle but important change – suddenly the corporate focus is on what small, incremental changes can be made that might ameliorate the risk, but which all too often cement the original problem firmly into all aspects of a business.

I am not saying for a moment that these may not be genuinely tough problems to solve – in a significant number they are. But repeatedly deferring the inevitable changes that need to be made very rarely generates the best outcomes over the longer term. So once again we have a problem of time scales.

A great example here is bank IT systems. Until quite recent years, many banking businesses around the world still used banking platforms based on 1970s technology and code. Indeed many still do. To put this into perspective, who still remembers the Tandy TRS-80 personal computer? Or the Commodore PET? These were both iconic computing devices of that time (both were released in 1977), and both were technically obsolete by the early 1980s. Since then we have had many generations of computer chips, sustained exponential increases in computing power, the revolution of the graphical user interface, the advent of the internet, the birth of mass mobile communication, and much, much more. Yet the functionality of the world's financial system still relies at least in part on technology that is now over 30 years out of date, very much because of the perceived risk and complexity of change.

Of course these systems will have to change eventually, and the costs and risks of doing so are unlikely to decrease. The sums involved are monstrous, with the world's largest banks spending many billions of dollars a year on system changes and developments, with costs that are substantially inflated because they are working with old inflexible systems. And so, for decades, these legacy systems have been preserved, enhanced and embellished, making the eventual systems transition more and more complex, and more and more risky.

GUILTY AS CHARGED: CHOOSING INCREMENTAL INEFFICIENCY

So why are these problems so common? Most businesses follow an orderly and practical business planning cycle. This involves building up annual and longer term budgets and development plans department by department, division by division, region by region. These inputs are added together to develop an overall group budget and medium term plan. This bottom-up approach is very logical, as it helps to ensure buy-in from the underlying businesses and management teams that will be expected to deliver on these budgets. But the approach can easily miss much bigger picture issues. Without a clear destination against which to assess the short term plans, the organisation can wander off course.

From time to time, a group level gap analysis may be carried out to highlight any variances between this bottom-up budgeting process, and medium to long term shareholder or market expectations. Again, this is useful as an early warning system in relation to profit generation. But it doesn't add any perspective on how the company can address the gap, or why shareholders' or market expectations are diverging from what the company thinks is possible. Even more importantly, it doesn't address at all whether the organisation is really headed in the right direction.

Faced with these challenges, every once a while a new CEO and her management consulting advisors will suggest a reorganisation, to refocus the business better on its "core customers" or "core markets" or "core products". As a result, there will very likely be changes to the order in which the micro business plans are prepared, drawn together and reported to senior management. But the same old incremental, organic business development continues.

Does this sound familiar? The evidence of these failings is widespread in both the Government and private sectors. In sector after sector, region after region, there are surprisingly few examples of companies or countries that materially outperform their direct competitors and peers in any significant or sustained manner. Before the howls of protest start, and a thousand "transform your company" business texts are hurled in my direction, let me quickly add that there are exceptions which prove this rule. But for every Apple or Samsung, there are dozens of entirely undistinguished peers and also-rans.

On a more positive note, the instincts of many people in the system are often right. Just as we knew on Steamy Windows that "something was wrong", bureaucrats and middle management around the world are nearly always pretty clear where the basic long term challenges lie. Unfortunately, they also know that the problems are too hard to solve, or that political and business leaders don't have the will or leverage to tack them, and that there is significantly more personal risk than reward in sticking their neck out to make decisive changes.

What's worse than this, there are too many examples of organisations, both in the private and Government sectors, that effectively lock in increasing inefficiency over time, as a result of a culture and approach based squarely on incremental, near term, bottom up planning.

CAN YOU HEAR YOUR COMPANY'S OWN DEATH KNELL?

Business history is littered with skeletons of once great companies that didn't notice the increasing risk of their own demise until far too late. Very few organisations feel comfortable exploring scenarios which involve their own business shrinking rapidly or failing completely within the near to medium term. The implied belief in longevity is arguably an instinctive and natural behaviour, as there are hundreds of years of corporate experience which show that nearly all larger organisations survive from year to year.

Nevertheless, over the longer term, most organisations die – very few remain industry leaders for fifty years at a time. So it is important for any organisation to think about when or in what circumstances its products and services might become irrelevant. This knowledge is incredibly valuable – particularly if the organisation is prepared to act on it. Most importantly, if your organisation is truly mindful of the circumstances in which it will become irrelevant, or is most likely to fail, it can plan for this eventuality and better recognise the threat should it emerge.

Of course corporate survivor bias means that we tend to forget the organisations which fail, especially if they do so slowly, reinforcing the collective corporate psyche which trusts in the ability to maintain status quo. This is one of the reasons why so few companies concern themselves with this type of existential risk analysis.

Much less excusable is when industry leaders treat young, creative, dynamic competitors with disdain, assuming that the hungry young mountain lion that has entered the park won't ever catch much prey. The emergence of new entrants, with new business models, new propositions and the energy of youth should act as an alarm call heard by all in the ecosystem.

Dramatic examples of the risk of believing in the status quo are found in many industries. Only a few years ago, Nokia was the mobile phone of choice for much of the world. Today its market value is 90% below its peak and it has sold its mobile business to Microsoft for just US$7 billion. In turn, it remains to be seen whether Microsoft can breathe life into this business, and build real market share in the pocket computer business (ie smartphones) to match its success in the PC and laptop segments.

Meanwhile Lehman Brothers and Bear Stearns were amongst the world's top dozen investment banks at the start of the year in which they failed. And Arthur Andersen was one of the world's five leading accounting practices when it was brought down by its involvement in the Enron scandal.

And of course closing a business when it reaches the end of its natural life need not be a failure. Indeed, the best way to maximise value for shareholders may well be to orchestrate an orderly wind down, rather than attempt to build an entirely new business out of remnants of a business that had been successful in a different world.

THAT'S A BEAUTIFUL MAP, BUT WHERE ARE WE GOING?

As any good navigator will tell you, all of this information is tremendously useful in assessing near term weather conditions and how to prepare and provision the ship. What it doesn't do, however, is set out the destination that you are hoping to reach. And without a destination, the course that is set day by day, month by month, year by year, will simply lead through a series of accidents to wherever the organisational, economic and financial winds blow you. You may get lucky, of course, and discover that your company is unexpectedly sitting on a gold mine. Far more likely, however, your company will find itself growing incrementally weaker, surrounded by new, stronger competitors, with better business models, better products (or worse, radically disruptive alternatives to your own products), more cost efficient operations, and employees who are energised by their company's achievements and sense of purpose.

If you are mesmerised by the complexity of change and innovation, how can you ever break out of this cycle of continuous small changes – changes that don't ever address the key issues? Above all else, you need a carefully chosen, and very clearly articulated, destination.

This concept of destination is absolutely critical. It is hugely more important than strategy per se, as strategy is simply the basic game plan for how you plan to reach the destination. Sticking with the navigational theme, here's a simple mnemonic "NORTH" which captures the essence of a great strategy.

- **New:** Your overall strategic destination needs to be big, bold and courageous enough to drive your organisation to a whole new level. In short, it needs to move you forward from where you are now to new (or different) heights, remembering that the status quo is simply not an option if you want to maintain competitive advantage over the near to medium term.

- **Opportunistic:** The right destination should help to ensure your organisation remains resilient and competitive as the commercial, economic and financing environment continues to change. With significant changes coming more and more rapidly, building resilience and flexibility into your organisations is becoming critically important in most industries. So a strong destination will be based not on historic market conditions, but will be forward looking, taking account of anticipated and realistic future market developments over the near to medium term.

- **Rousing**: Your strategy isn't really for you, nor is it for your Board and management team. Even your shareholders are not the most important community here. More than anything, your destination must be inspiring for your entire workforce and for your customers and for the community in which you operate. You should be confident to share your strategic destination publicly – after all you will distinguish your organisation not by the brilliance of the destination, but by how rapidly you achieve it. If your customers and your workforce and the broader community support what you are seeking to achieve, you will have a strong following wind to help you on your way.

- **Tangible**: Yes, you must be able to describe your destination clearly and you must be able to get there. No-one ever climbed to the clouds ten miles above Everest, so your ultimate destination must be somewhere that your organisation can actually reach within the medium to long term.

- **Hard**: Although your destiny should be achievable, it shouldn't be too easy. Indeed it should be genuinely challenging to achieve, so that every part of the organisation is truly stretched to achieve it. Anything less, and you are simply planning to be an also-ran.

CRYSTAL BALLS 101: BUILDING A TRULY INSIGHTFUL FINANCIAL MODEL

Once you have established a clear destination, one of the fundamental challenges is simply to develop a sufficiently robust set of financial analytics that you can use as a proper foundation for longer term decision-making. And by long term, I mean at least 20 years, not just the five to ten years often found in corporate decision-making. One conceptual challenge is the approach that you take to uncertainty. Developing a base case and then exploring upside and downside scenarios is a very blunt instrument, and becomes blunter by the year as the pace of change accelerates. As we explored earlier, you shouldn't try to simplify uncertainty to a few variables, rather you should find ways to embrace it within your financial analytics.

If you can build really robust financial analytics, the more obvious risks inherent in maintaining the status quo will become clear. So will inconsistencies in assumptions buried in your organisation's medium to long term assumptions.

Going back to the planning cycle above, hopefully the management forecasts will be subject to some top-down analytical review, to identify fundamental inconsistencies in underlying assumptions. All too often, however, I see examples where top line growth is forecast to accelerate at the same time as significant cost efficiencies are being implemented and capital investment budgets cut. This of course translates to impressive growth in profitability, and correspondingly high implied (but entirely theoretical) discounted cash flow valuations. Unsurprisingly, these valuations are very rarely realised in practice.

So the challenge is, however, to make sure that there is sufficient discipline and financial expertise to develop a parallel top down set of projections. This book has deliberately stayed away from the more technical areas of finance, but good financial modelling is such an incredibly important tool and in this context there are two areas it is very helpful to understand.

The first area relates to the design and architecture of financial models – ie how they are built up and how they work.

- At the outset, you must ensure that the mechanics and architecture of the model mirror the way the business actually works in real life. As an example, think about the banking sector. If the interest rate charged to customers is set as a spread on top of the central bank base rate, then you should have a forecast for the central bank base rate, and show separately the forecasts for the lending spreads that will be achieved. What you mustn't do is just insert forecasts for the effective lending rate to the customer. If you do, your model will hide one of the fundamental variables for the business – ie the central bank base rate. This variable is, of course, entirely outside the bank's control. This example may sound reasonably obvious, but I see plenty of examples where businesses make directly analogous mistakes in the construction of their internal forecasts;

- You must also ensure that all the input data is robustly tied back to a reliable source – preferably the audited financial statements. This is a basic but critical discipline, and it is amazing how often you uncover inconsistencies of fundamental importance. In addition, the longer the history that can be gathered in a consistent format (ie without changes in accounting policies or disclosures), the better. This provides a much better sense of the longer term direction of the business, and whether recent performance is in line with that history, represents a near term aberration, or indeed reflects a much longer term trend; and

–   Finally, if you want to use the model as a basis for making investment decisions, it needs to be a fully integrated, three way model. In other words, it needs to include not only a profit and loss account but also a detailed balance sheet and cash flow statement, all linked together and reconciled so that the three move precisely in tandem. The simple reason for this is that, without this information, you won't know what return on capital you are achieving or whether the business is generating or consuming cash as it grows (or shrinks). Once again, this sounds all too obvious, but amazingly often larger businesses do not have accurate or reliable balance sheet information at a divisional or sub-segment level. In most cases this will completely undermine the reliability and usefulness of a financial model as a decision-making tool, as the companies concerned will have no way to determine whether the business in question is generating an adequate return on capital.

As a practical tip, if you or your advisors have a "standard" model, then in nearly all cases the best thing will be to throw this out and start from scratch. One simple reason for doing this is that whoever builds the model will gain a much deeper understanding of the business in question than they can ever gain from simply typing historic figures into a standard template model. Another is that nearly every business has its particular vagaries which are best examined explicitly, rather than being shoe-horned into an ill-fitting standard framework.

And, if you know what you are doing, this doesn't need to take long. A decent financial analyst can build a detailed, multi division, properly integrated three-way financial model in under a day. With the right approach, even an extremely complex business can be modelled in a few days. This is an incredibly minute investment for something so important. Building financial models of this nature has long been a passion, and I still believe there is no better way to understand how the profits and cash returns from business are really generated than to work your way through a really well-designed financial model.

Of course those that are familiar with building such models will know that there can be challenges in ensuring that everything in the model balances, in an accounting sense, and of course standard models avoid this problem. Nevertheless, the advantage of toughing out this stage of the process is that very often you will find that the causes of any balancing errors in the model represent unusual aspects of the business in question or how it accounts for its results.

In my experience, the only exception to this bespoke approach would be if you operate in a sector where there are many identical companies, which manage their businesses in very similar ways and report in a completely standardised format, and you already have an ideal model to hand which you understand well. In practice this is very rare – I've only ever benefited from it in Japan, which has over a hundred listed regional banks, all of which had very similar savings and mortgage business activities and reported in more or less identical formats.

That's it for corporate finance 101. What matters even more is how you use it once it's built. If you are part of the Board or management team reviewing one, there are three key factors to look out for that will clearly differentiate genuinely useful projections from all the rest.

- The first is to ensure that any scenario being considered is a "realistic" one. This may sound subjective, but in practice a very good guide is to ensure that all financial ratios and operational performance metrics throughout the model move in an internally consistent manner. As an example, dramatic growth is unlikely to be achieved without a corresponding increase in marketing effort. Conversely, a slump in revenues will likely be offset by significant reductions in some areas of cost in the business. Significant balance sheet effects – such as changes in working capital compared to revenues – are unlikely to continue over long periods of time. In other words, the objective is to ensure that any internal inconsistencies in the model are removed. The best way to do this is to examine the widest possible range of ratios and similar financial metrics and to consider whether they all look reasonable;

- The second is to ensure that the model has few enough input assumptions so that each of them has a material impact on overall outcomes, including valuation (you can have as many outputs as you like). There is obviously a tension between this requirement, and the desire for the model to provide a realistic image of how the business actually works. With too much complexity and too many inputs, however, you rapidly reach a point at which none of the inputs has any meaningful impact, making insightful sensitivity analysis genuinely challenging and thus undermining the power of a good top down model. For a more sophisticated approach, you can of course utilise Monte Carlo simulations to explore a much wider range of scenarios, put together in a statistically meaningful manner, and this is by far the most robust approach;

- The third is to look far enough out in the future so that the period of explicit financial projections addresses a meaningful part of the company's overall value. As an example, a three to five year forecast is pretty useless for most companies, as it will account for much less than half the overall value. Of course, making longer term forecasts is more challenging than near term forecasts, but this is no reason to try to avoid tackling these issues head on. Where uncertainty regarding future outcomes is high, techniques such as Monte Carlo simulations can again be used to explore risks in a statistically robust manner. As an aside, these techniques are widely used in the scientific and engineering communities, but are hardly ever seen in Boardrooms or in the hands of their strategy or investment banking advisers.

This brings me neatly back to timescales. These longer term forecasts will often highlight further areas of inconsistency in a company's thinking. This may be as simple as assuming that exceptionally high returns can be maintained for decades to come. This is another way of saying that competitive advantage can be maintained over very long, multi-decadal time periods. Such assumptions need to be considered very carefully, as even natural monopolies have a habit of being successfully attacked by disruptive innovators if the profit pool is large enough – Skype and long distance telephone calls is just one example.

THE PERILS OF LINEAR THINKING

These basic tools provide a critical starting point, but they are only a tool in the decision-making process. There are, of course, numerous books to help you "transform your business" (my quotes), many of them filled with practical ideas and suggestions. So why do so many large companies struggle to outperform their peers?

One of the most fundamental challenges is that business culture and problem solving is essentially linear in nature. We start from where we are now, and wonder how we can improve and grow. This mindset is – for some good reasons – hard wired into the corporate planning cycle and many other features of business life. Aspects of this reflect a Neanderthal single-minded archetype of focussing on the very immediate task at hand – hunting and killing a mammoth. Once set in motion, such thinking and processes are hard to stop. Even the words "business improvement" build in the implication that "better" must be "better than now" rather than "completely different".

But the world we live in is much more complex than this, and this complexity seems to be increasing exponentially day by day. The accessibility of existing human knowledge, automation of discovery and invention, dramatic increases in interconnectivity of people and ideas each catalyse yet more rapid change in personal desires, social needs, business opportunities and the economic landscape. A surprising number of the world's largest companies are disruptive innovators who didn't exist twenty years ago.

With this in mind, companies need to embrace the concept that doing things differently may in fact be safer than doing them the same, especially when viewed over a time frame of five years or more. This principal is easy to describe, but is likely to be extremely tough in practice given the cultural barriers to adopting a much more dynamic approach to business development. The most challenging part of this is that many millennia of human and animal experience has taught that doing things the same way as before is safer than experimentation. Human and animal instinct reflects exactly this learning. With the pace of change continuing to increase, however, there will soon come an inflection point when change becomes safer than the status quo.

This is a truly dramatic change – one that requires a fundamental reprogramming of corporate survival instincts. And common sense should tell us that the time for this change is coming very near. The last decade has seen numerous very large businesses transformed from leaders to bleeders in a matter of years, a graphic demonstration of how dangerous the status quo has become in some industries.

If you and your organisation are able to embrace the notion that change is safer than inertia, this will give you an important protection against complacency. One fundamental challenge for incumbent industry leaders is that they frequently struggle to imagine that the fabric of their operational world can ever be different. Even if the organisations have not succumbed to the supremacy gene, they may still be blinkered regarding the potential for the emergence of a new business paradigm.

As a simple example, I was talking in 2012 with a senior executive from a world-leading petroleum company about the potential advantages of new types of cars. We talked in particular about Tesla's all electric Model S and explored a few rational comparisons. For example, the Model S is cheap to refuel and can be filled at home. It has much better, more flexible, on board technology, not to mention exceptional acceleration and more storage space. Eventually the executive said, "But people like petrol!".

This hit me like a bolt of lightning. Of course, very few people really like petrol. Seriously, how many people do you know who keep a jar on the mantelpiece? Or use it as a perfume? Or head to the pump to meet their friends. What people really do like most of all is the convenience of being self-sufficient when it comes to transport. They like that their vehicle is relatively cheap to run and that it is easy to fill up. And they like that they can drive for a few days – or even a week – without having to refuel. In this sense petrol driven cars are better than horses in most respects, and they are much less polluting (just google "horses cars pollution New York" if you're not familiar with this story.

But people don't actually like petrol. Emerging electric car technologies are providing vehicles that are cheaper to run, can easily be refuelled at home, and have a range of 500 kilometres or more – enough for a week for a typical urbanite. And in a complete challenge to the status quo, Tesla is offering free refuelling on longer trips – using solar powered recharge stations, with zero marginal cost of power. And remember, in remote locations where there's sunshine, it's much, much easier to refuel using solar power than it is to deliver tanker-loads of petrol. It is amazing what is possible if you can truly re-imagine your industry freed from the constraints of the accidental present.

IGNORING THE "NO" IN INNOVATION

So, to thrive in an increasingly complex world, you must take a much more flexible, open-mind approach to most aspects of corporate and business decision-making. If you spend too much time worshipping at the altar of economic rationalism, you will miss many opportunities to create substantial value, and you will progressively build much greater risk into your organisation.

Traditional valuation methodologies, with their strong emphasis on the near term, hide the biggest opportunities and the biggest threats.

There's also potential for significant social benefit from this approach. In our personal lives, we naturally place a much greater emphasis on the longer term – this is illustrated very clearly by the thought experiment about discounting your family in Chapter 2. Better longer term decision-making offers the opportunity to combine greater economic benefit with improved social prosperity, in part by avoiding all the costs and inefficiencies of building businesses and economies through a never-ending series of short term plans.

You also have to be able to free yourself of preconceptions about what will determine success and be on your guard against single track, linear thinking which forces you down a path towards incremental inefficiency. You have to make sure that you and your organisation are not suffering from the supremacy gene. And you have to believe that by thinking differently, you can find a better, safer, more profitable, more exciting way to serve your customers.

There's a well-known problem solving algorithm in mathematics – the Feynman Problem-Solving Algorithm. It goes like this. "Write down the problem. Think very hard about it. Write down the answer." The real beauty of this approach for me has always been that it embodies very gracefully the sense of being unconstrained by your starting point. Indeed I explicitly add an extra step at the beginning: "Think really hard about the problem!". In many situations, the most challenging part of solving a problem is to be able to enunciate the problem you are trying solve the right way at the outset, before you know the answer. This is tremendously important, as it is the question that frames how people think about and attempt to solve the problem. This mental freedom is the absolute catalyst for successful innovation and organisational creativity. This frees you from starting from where you are today.

For businesses and organisations grappling with significant change, the fundamental steps are similarly simple. You must cast off the chains of corporate process and put on the inventor's cloak of invisibility, so that you can travel in your mind to places that you might never previously have dared visit. It works like this:

- Forget where you are, and your current products and services and strengths and weaknesses;

- Dare to imagine future products and distribution channels and manufacturing processes that bear no relation to the present day and which really give your customer what they want;

- Walk backwards from this ideal end destination, to figure out what you would have to achieve to get there.

Often the route to radical development may be deceptively simple. Imagine if IBM had asked: "What if we design computers as output devices, not as input devices?" You wouldn't really need a keyboard, would you? You'd need good data transmission speeds (to download all that data). At some point TVs might become much less relevant. You'd want to be able tap a button to buy things. So you'd imagine the tablet. Of course quite a few leading technology companies did do precisely this, but it was Apple and Steve Jobs that combined all the features into a beautifully-designed product that lit up the desires of a billion people around the world (the iPad).

There are, of course, many other examples. Frequently inventors, innovators and entrepreneurs are surrounded by people who say "it won't work...". The naysayers may well offer reasoning that appears plausible or even commercially sound. But the simple truth is the world's greatest inventions were not created by people who sought out the "*No*" in innovation. The great innovators were those who believed that they had found a new and better way to solve a problem or serve a need. Over the centuries, many of them discovered that bringing their inventions to life – first in theory and then in practice – was much more challenging than they might have imagined. And frequently they learned that the voices of the incumbents were much louder, and much better financed, than voices of the new. But no matter how far away the destination, or how hard the journey, inventors and innovators and entrepreneurs have all realised one thing. The long term starts tomorrow, so you'd better begin now.

10.   Epilogue: Saving Jorgen's frog:

WHERE DID ALL THE GROWTH GO?

Around the world, people who expected to be at the peak of their earning capacity as they hit their forties and fifties are working harder than ever before, often for lower real rewards than earlier in their careers.   Ten or fifteen years earlier, generation X was contemplating retiring at 50, safe in the knowledge that they were generating far more capital than their parents. Now retirement seems further away than ever. They are struggling to educate their children, pay their aging parents' medical bills and still find a way to save for the future. Their parent's once well-funded retirement plans have been eaten away by a decade of low returns, not to mention cost of living increases and rapidly rising healthcare costs. In a true sign of the times, hardly anyone seems to have the time for an old-fashioned mid-life crisis.

Meanwhile retirees are wondering what happened to their corporate pensions and life savings. Bank deposits and their bond equivalents are paying record low returns and they simply cannot afford to provide the same financial support to their children and grandchildren that was afforded to them.

Meanwhile generations Y and Z are much less concerned about longer term growth. Although they are disillusioned by the corporate world and job prospects, they have immersed themselves in the moment, and are much less obsessed than the predecessors with the need to accumulate capital, particularly residential property. So they spend their income on mobile phones and fashion and holidays and don't worry too much about the future.

For everyone, there is a common underlying question that must be answered. Will it all work out all right in the end?

Without significant changes in the way decisions are made, it is hard to see that it will. Just as companies have discovered that extreme leverage will find you out in the end, so surely must excessive national debt impinge significantly on long term economic growth. At the simplest level, greater national debt means that a greater proportion of current spending must go to pay for the pleasures of the past. This results in a significant transfer of wealth from future generations to the present, before those generations even have the right to vote. Of course the sting may yet come in the tail for generation X, if welfare and retirement provision is reined back significantly just at the time when they are heading into retirement.

And, just as many Western economies have borrowed from the future to pay for the past in a financial sense, the same is true of historic use of petro-chemicals for fuel. If the world had paid heed to the analysis included in "Limits to Growth" – and indeed the writings of many other academics – only a modest rate of change to use of fossil fuels would now be needed to keep global warming below two degrees. Instead, we have almost completely used up the limits of carbon dioxide that can be added to the atmosphere without creating dramatic climate change, and there are still only limited signs of real action being taken to address these challenges.

These are both terrible legacies to leave future generations – and the significant majority of those who are writing these legacies today will live to look into the eyes of the children and grandchildren that will have to bear them in 2030 and beyond.

The only solution to challenges this significant is to remember that the long term starts tomorrow, and to seek out different, more positive perspectives on where opportunities lie. The goal must be to meet these challenges in a way that creates better outcomes than might ever have been possible if the challenges hadn't been there in the first place.

SAVING JORGEN'S FROG

The genesis of this book was a series of discussions in Sydney, Australia, at the end of 2011 with Professor Jorgen Randers, one of the authors of the seminal "Limits to Growth" study. Professor Randers was leading Cambridge University's "Sustainability Leadership Programme" in Sydney, which I had the pleasure of attending and contributing to as a presenter with my colleague Julian King PhD. These conversations explored systemic issues that posed a material threat to the sustainability of the corporate, consumer and political ecosystem in which we live. Inevitably, they set me thinking. With all the advances in management theory, and financial analysis, and information and communications, how could the world economy have got so rapidly to such a dark place?

As early as 1798, the demographer The Rev Thomas Malthus had set out a series of concerns and predictions regarding the longer term threats posed by unbounded growth in his paper entitled *"An Essay on the Principle of Population"*. Others before and after had raised similar concerns, but in the fifty year boom which followed the two world wars, these concerns seemed far-fetched. Bearded eco-warriors chained themselves to fences and shouted that the world was doomed, but the petrol kept pumping, innovation continued, share prices rose, and nearly everyone was happy.

Following the Second World War, global populations had begun to rise more steeply, reflecting dramatic improvements in diet, medicine and healthcare in both the developed and emerging markets.   In 1970, the Club of Rome, a global think tank consisting of current and former Heads of State, UN bureaucrats, high-level politicians and government officials, diplomats, scientists, economists, and business leaders from around the globe commissioned research from MIT to explore potential threats to long term economic prosperity imposed by the world's simple physical limitations.

The authors used system dynamics theory and a computer model called "World3," to analyse potential world development between 1900 and 2100. The scenarios showed how population growth and natural resource use interacted to impose limits to industrial growth. This was a controversial idea at the time – in 1972, the world's population and economy were still well within the boundaries that define sustainable world development and economic growth. This meant that there was still a pathway for safe global growth over the near term, and time to explore how best to manage the longer term challenges.

The findings from the research were published in "Limits to Growth".   In this book, the authors described the potential relationships between world population, industrialization, pollution, food production and resource depletion. The analysis highlighted the concern that the world had reasonably clear system limits regarding the level of population and economic growth that could readily be sustained. This included resources that have been widely discussed in popular media over the forty years since the book was first written, including petroleum. It also addressed other system limits – including the effects of carbon dioxide emissions from fossil fuels and significant restrictions on some parts of the world's food system, including fish stocks. Two of the scenarios indicated "overshoot and collapse" of the global system by the mid to latter parts of the 21st century.

On the 20th anniversary of the publication of Limits to Growth, the team updated Limits in a book called Beyond the Limits. Already in the 1990s there was compelling evidence that humanity was moving deeper into unsustainable territory. Since then, a number of updates to the research have been published, all confirming that the underlying logics and primary conclusions remain reasonable. Recently, Australia's Commonwealth Scientific and Industrial Research Organisation published a paper that compared the predictions made in 1972 with thirty years of real world data. The report found that changes in industrial production, food production and pollution are all in line with the book's predictions of economic and societal collapse in the 21st century.

The discussions in Sydney provided a strong juxtaposition between the pessimism of Professor Randers, who had seen so many initiatives fail around the world, and more optimistic contributors to the debate. More than anything, my mind turned to the cautionary tale of the boiling frog. If you drop him in hot water, he will jump right out again. But if you put him in cold water, and turn the heat up slowly, he will quietly just cook.

We spoke about Jorgen's frog – a metaphor for human decision-making. Professor Randers' concern is that human decision-making is – and will remain – dominated by a short-term focus. This pre-occupation with the immediate future will lead directly to the sub-optimal and entirely avoidable futures described in both "Limits to Growth" and his most recent book 2052. Thus the "frog" in Jorgen's view is "the market liberalist world view". As long as humanity maintains this world view, we will stay in the water and be cooked.

So it seems to be with the world's system limits. Intuitively we know that there must be such limits, and it seems entirely logical that there must only be so many people who can be fed from the land, or eat fish from the sea. As for climate change, just like the frog, we have been dropped in cool water and the temperature is only increasing slowly. Unlike the frog, we ought to be smart enough to be wary of the danger and able to investigate our surroundings. And if we do, we can tell that climate change is happening, as there is strong empirical evidence all around us, not to mention the never-ending stream of record extreme weather events.

So I left the discussion wondering what could be done to save Jorgen's frog. The more I examined the underlying issues, the more they seemed to provide fascinating parallels with the world's corporate, economic and financial challenges.

THE LONG TERM STARTS TOMORROW (PART 2)

The simplest challenge is that we need to find ways to make short term decisions that will lead to the best long term outcomes. Despite the obsession with the near term, the large majority of the value of any business remains in the future as the years go by – typically at least half, if not more. So every day, the decisions that are made and actions that are taken conspire to frame the future for the organisation in question. Every single step is a step towards a destination, whether or not that destination has been consciously chosen or is simply going to be the outcome of a corporate random walk. This is what I mean by saying that the long term starts tomorrow. Ultimately the successful business will make every single decision count positively towards long term success.

So what changes do businesses need to make?

The age of financial rationalism has brought many benefits, but it has also conspired to focus businesses on near term profits and maximising their share prices in the short term, all too often at the expense of long term value. This obsession with spot values and the immediate future has been instrumental in many of the most significant corporate disasters of the last thirty years. Meanwhile the opposite is also true, with the companies that have created $100 billion dollar market values in under a decade having been very clearly focussed on building businesses that will be profitable in the long term, even if this came at the expense of short term profits.

An obsession with financial modelling and, dare I say it, a highly male dominated business culture, has led to business philosophies that are imbued with linear logic. The financial appraisal techniques taught in business schools and employed by companies and their investment bank advisers have barely changed in twenty years. Despite their intricacy, these models simply do not embrace complexity. At best, they explore a range of scenarios and use simple sensitivity tables to flex a couple of inputs.

Very rarely do you see statistically robust analysis of likely uncertainties in key inputs combined with mathematical investigation of inter-relationships between the various key inputs to the model. But you will know it if you see it, because all of a sudden a much wider range of possible outcomes will be on the table. You may not like all the findings, but they will look much more like the real world and will provoke a much more meaningful debate around the boardroom or cabinet table.

There are many artificial barriers to a company pursuing strategies that will optimise growth and profitability. These may come within the company itself through business model and operational structure, or may be imposed from outside as a result of regulation or industry structure. These are the chains of the free market, and you have to find a way to cast them off. Whatever the cause, any organisation seeking to differentiate itself from its peers needs to have the courage to break the mould, whether through unilateral action or by working with peers and other interested parties to effect change.

Much more serious than these is the supremacy gene, an internal enemy that is usually far more dangerous than external competitors. The weakness is easy for outsiders to diagnose, but it is much harder for industry leaders themselves to accept that they have been afflicted by this condition. Once an organisation has reached a position where it believes in its unassailable corporate superiority, reversing the inevitable subsequent decline is incredibly challenging.

Like most conditions of the mind, unless the patient can recognise the problems and willingly seek treatment, the chances of a successful cure are low. And the larger the organisation, the more people are involved, and the more severe the therapy must be. At the least, significant change of the Board and senior management will be necessary in most cases, and indeed it may be that the electric shock treatment of a takeover is the only way to re-invigorate the business.

At an even deeper level, your own perceptions colour your thinking about what is possible and when it can be achieved, often in an irrational and unhelpful manner. To avoid these traps for the imagination, you need to become conscious of how problems are being framed and the constraints that this imposes on the solutions. As with any complex challenge, the greatest impediment is most often simply being able to enunciate clearly what the problem really is, in a way that doesn't limit the types of solution that you might contemplate.

All too often in business and in Government, problems are examined in the most minute detail. But the more closely you inspect them, the more likely you are to miss the big, simple solution. There are endless examples of "Why didn't I think of that" businesses and products and services. Whilst some have been enabled by market or technological development, in many cases someone has simply come up with a new and better solution to a well-established problem by starting their thinking from a completely different perspective. My favourite example of this is airlines that use both the back and the front door to board planes – unsurprisingly, it cuts boarding and disembarking times by more or less 50%, saving customers time and improving aircraft utilisation rates.

To launch a new period of sustained improvement in living standards (and note I am not suggesting that this must necessarily require "growth"), we need to abandon the false gods of financial rationalism. This does not mean we have to give up rigorous financial analysis and appraisal. Rather it means that we must find ways to assess the strategic, commercial and financial viability of projects that do not overemphasise short term returns at the expense of longer term value creation. We must recognise that, however beguiling these financial sirens have been, they have led corporations and governments onto the rocks of short-termism and have inhibited the pursuit of solutions that would have had much better impacts over the longer term.

How will we find our way in this brave new world beyond financial rationalism? As with any journey, the most important starting point is to set a very clear long term strategic destination. This destination needs to be chosen so that it steers your company or organisation towards a stronger, more sustainable long term market position. The destination needs to be effectively communicated to your customers and employees and shareholders, and every decision along the way must advance you towards that destination. This clarity of purpose will help eliminate many distractions and will ensure that every short term decision is aligned with the right long term outcome.

SMALL SELFISH STEPS

All this begins to sound quite easy, until you start to think about how you can influence large organisations, let alone industry competitors or other stakeholders to join you on the journey. How on earth do you encourage others to follow the same path, when many of them are (at least for the near term!) very much enjoying the comfort of their current position. Indeed many of these leaders may care little about the outcomes, as they sleep at night safe in the knowledge that they have a large pension to comfort them in their retirement.

In a wonderful stroke of outright co-incidence, the Sustainability Leadership programme that I attended also included a segment from a leading soil scientist. Like others who participated, I was surprised to learn of the incredible complexity of even very small pieces of soil, let alone to see the extraordinary images that he and his team had been able to make using electron microscopy of soil structures (something which no-one had thought to do before!). The discussions turned rapidly to the forces of evolution, and how changes in large, complex systems could be - indeed almost always are - driven by small selfish steps. In other words, the future of an organism can be driven significantly in a particular direction so long as the small, individual actions required by the individual components of the organism are very much in their self-interest.

The parallels with the corporate and government sectors were immediately obvious. Any fight to change an entire belief system, or to change an entire organisation that knows that it is a world market leader, is surely doomed to failure. But if you could find small ways to influence the thinking of such organisations - or at least to stimulate some form of momentary greed - then perhaps you really could start a chain reaction.

About the same time, I read George Lakoff's book "Don't Think of an Elephant", which highlighted the potential to explore "small selfish steps" campaigns at a metaphysical level as well. Simply by framing questions in a particular manner, or from a slightly different stand point, you can unleash an entire chain of questions and thinking that lead the target inescapably to a new level of understanding.

I still remember one of my earlier experiments with this tactic, at a business lunch for some 500 people. Towards the end of a Q&A session on the outlook for Australia's economy with one of the most senior members of Australia's Reserve Bank, I asked the following question:

"What impact do you think China's policies on climate change will have on Australia's long term growth?"

The moment the answer started, I knew I was on to a winner. "I'm no expert on China's policies on climate change, but....". The point was made – and was apparent to many people in the room. In particular, everyone knew that resources exports were critical to Australia's economy. Everyone knew that China was the most significant driver of marginal demand for Australia's resources exports. And once the question had been asked, it would have been hard for most people not to wonder whether China actually had policies on climate change (which of course it does). So it was obvious that a senior representative of the Reserve Bank really should be an expert on China's policies on climate change. Indeed, maybe this was the most important single factor that would determine the medium to long term economic outlook for Australia.

And here's the point – the objective of the question was nothing to do with Australia's economic outlook. The primary focus was to highlight just how important action on climate change by other countries was going to be to Australia's future, irrespective of Australia's own decisions on adaptation and change.

We will never know precisely what impact this question had on the thinking of people who attended that particular lunch. This is the challenge with the small selfish steps strategy, as it is very hard to see cause and effect. Nevertheless I was happy to discover some months later that the Reserve Bank was singularly better informed on China's climate change policies.

You should try the same approach in your own organisation. If there is a transformational change that you believe is important, and the business culture won't let you engage in the right debate, then focus first on shifting the way the debate is framed. And as you do this, take courage that it is much more rewarding to stand up and catalyse change, than to sit in a back room and watch your company die.

EMBRACE MADNESS!

If you want to change your business, or your industry, or your country, you need to be bold. Great results will never be achieved by taking the back seat and hoping that the driver takes you to the right place. So to close this book, I offer you these inspirational words from Frank Danieli, a much younger colleague that I had the pleasure of working with at Pottinger.

"Great companies stand out from the rest. They are leaders who drive the direction of entire industry sectors. They are more highly valued than their competitors. Their customers embrace them and loyally support them through thick and thin. And every management team wants their company to be seen as one of the greats.

But what does it really take to be a great company? The management books written on great companies refer to "competitive advantage", "sources of differentiation" and "customer centricity." The problem is that this jargon refers to ends, not means. Competitive advantage is not an ingredient for success, it is an outcome of the process of achieving market leadership. True leaders have several points of differentiation, but that description provides no insight into how a company goes about differentiating itself. Being "close to the customer" is a feature of great organisations, but what did they actually do to become customer centric?

We say forget management 101. The secret is culture. Great organisations have "maverick" cultures. They are prepared to step out of line and change the rules of the game. They stand out from the rest because they believe in doing things differently and looking at the world in unique ways. You won't find the characteristics of these organisations in any textbook or MBA course, but you will see them if you take a look at the companies you admire.

Here are five things we see in the iconic innovators of today.

Embrace madness! Great companies equate madness with brilliance. They seek out wildly innovative and creative new ideas about their industry, their customers, their products and the world generally. These companies don't just push the boundaries; they redraw them. Sound easy enough? Think again. It takes extraordinary courage to embrace madness. To stare down the barrel of a global industry and say, with unwavering confidence, "You're doing it wrong!" is incredibly brave. But to be bold enough to rip up the rule book and say, "You're not just doing it wrong, you're playing the wrong game!" is something else entirely. Mavericks can do this because they aren't afraid of being denounced as mad.

Throw out the systems! Creative innovation doesn't just happen overnight. You need to nurture ideas and allow them to drift to the surface where they can be captured and acted upon. How do great companies do this? What special systems and procedures do they have to get their creative juices flowing? The answer may surprise you. Great companies thrive on the individuality, imagination and flair of every one of their people. They don't have a system to do this. In fact, they shun systems and procedures that turn their employees into cogs, whose role is to turn the same wheel, the same way, every day – even when they are "innovating." Freed from restrictive systems and inflexible procedures, thinking becomes more fluid and organisations become more dynamic. People are empowered, and so long as the culture prioritises a focus on working towards a shared vision, perpetual innovation becomes the norm. When an organisation throws out the systems, it will no longer be encumbered by legacy or accepted ways of

192

doing things. People will be at liberty to ask, "Why is something done this way?" and "Can we do it a better way?". Everyone in the organisation will be willing to scrap something that isn't working and start again. The organisation's products and services will become more elegant and more refined. This is why great companies appear to be "customer centric." They surprise their customers and clients because they are always looking for better ways of doing things and never settle for "good enough."

Look the other way! Great companies have an extraordinary ability to find untapped opportunities. They see possibilities that others do not and are able to dodge risks that steamroll their competitors. The leaders of these companies appear to have an uncanny ability to see the future. They somehow just know that it is time to invent a whole new market for a whole new product or to innovate in a way that doubles their market share. However, the way they do this is deceptively simple. General George S. Patton once said, "if everyone is thinking alike, then somebody isn't thinking." That is what great companies do: they look where others are not. Great companies look left when their competitors are looking right While it seems simple in theory, it is extremely hard to execute. People tend to gravitate toward the pack. They don't like to take the risk to step out and be the outsider, even if just for a short time. Another reason is that if the culture isn't right, the company just won't be able to look in a different direction. The concept of bounded rationality states that people can only make decisions based on what they currently know and are exposed to. This can apply to companies. If they don't have a culture that encourages lateral thinking and the generation of unique, creative ideas, they can't possibility think outside the box. They get tunnel vision and miss fantastic opportunities to grow.

Be right, as well as different! Of course, great companies know that just being different isn't a successful strategy in business. That is why traditional management texts that assert the need to find your "sources of *differentiation" are not truly helpful. You need to be right, as well as different. There needs to be a real value case for why doing something a different way will actually work. That doesn't mean you restrict ideas because of what your competitors are doing or the way things are traditionally done. It means you create an open and collaborative environment to mix, shake and stir ideas without inhibitions. People must have the licence to challenge each other and debate new ideas openly and honestly to find the best approach. Collaboration is about enhancing ideas and laying the foundation for new perspectives. So nobody's ideas, not even the most senior management, can be off-limits. And 'being right' is judged not by today's frame of reference, but by looking forward to the world the organisation wants to win in tomorrow.*

Value your vision more than the bottom line! There's an old adage that goes something like, "Why are you in business? To make a profit." It's wrong. The very best companies succeed not by focusing primarily on higher profits, better multiples or larger market capitalisations, but by a passionate drive to bring their vision into reality. The bottom line should be looked at as a facilitator of a company's vision. It can be a useful yardstick to measure progress and even a recognition that a company is doing the right thing. But vision should never take a back seat to the bottom line. A company's vision defines who it really is and what it really stands for. When a great vision is brought to life, it is truly valuable. In actual fact, it is worth more than can ever be achieved when higher value, a better multiple or more profits are the goal. Apple is the purest example of this. The company made its name at the dawn of the computer revolution by challenging everything that industry stood for at the time. It brought the graphic user interface and the mouse to market, when others simply couldn't see the value of those innovations. It was flexible and nimble, with a vision to create products that changed people's worlds – like "the computer for the rest of us," the Macintosh. But then, in 1985, the Board *fired Steve Jobs and Apple lost its focus. It became driven by profits, not vision. Its management style changed from being customer and product oriented to be sales oriented. And the company suffered. But in 1997, Steve Jobs was returned to the helm of Apple and took it from a $3 billion company on the verge of bankruptcy to the world's most valuable company today, valued at over US$590 billion. Incredibly, he did this without it ever being his goal. Jobs' obsession was not with market value. Instead, he had an outright fascination with the creative process, a passion for challenging the norm and an insatiable desire to change the world one device at a time. His secret was to rekindle Apple's maverick culture and empower its people who "bled in six colours" (a reference to Apple's famous coloured logo in its early years). By refocusing Apple on who it really was and what it really stood for, Jobs brought Apple's original vision back to life. Today, being part of Apple in any way – whether it be as a customer, employee, supplier or shareholder – is considered a symbol that you too share Apple's identity and sense of purpose. This is why Apple's fanatical customers line up for days just to get their hands on the next new product. They too live and breathe the vision.*

And that's the real point. Organisational culture is not set in stone. Any organisation can become a maverick at any time if it is prepared to throw out the rule book and craft a completely different culture. Truly great companies are bold enough to look at the world in fresh, new and entirely different ways. If they need to, they'll reinvent not only themselves, but their entire industry. They're mavericks and that's what makes them great."